<u>**Digging Deeper: A Soul Sea**</u>

The Lord allowed me to write this Interruption. I had NO intentions on writing a Bible Study. I had passed the Louisiana Bar Examination and was ready to practice law. However, GOD interrupted those plans – He saw fit that I would not be employed until this Bible Study and my autobiography had been put on paper.

I first wrote an autobiography and still found myself unemployed. I would go to morning Bible Study at my church, Franklin Avenue Baptist Church. Morning Bible Study was taught by Pastor Gary Mack. I would also attend other services and bible studies held at FABC. I also attended an all women's Bible Study entitled "Armor of God" facilitated by first lady Luter (and Priscilla Shirer). That is where I received the inspiration for the second part of this Bible Study.

It was during my period of interruption that God spoke clear to me – giving me specific instructions to follow. I grew so close to God during that period – thus, this very Bible Study is one of the results. I am thankful to God and I pray it blesses you tremendously.

Although you can engage in this Bible Study at any time of the year, it was prepared for the final 13-weeks of the year (October 1 to December 31). Again, you can engage at any time of the year.

At the end of the book, you will find Memory Verses for each week of the year. This is another way to dig deeper and search your soul as you become closer to God.

Part I – Fruit of the Spirit

During the first nine weeks, we will look at the Fruit of the Holy Spirit. Knowing The Fruit of the Holy Spirit is crucial in our walk with Christ because it helps us lead a life like Christ. The Fruit of the Holy Spirit helps us to respond (like Christ) to certain situations in our lives. For example, when we do not know how to treat a person, we remember that the Bible tells us to love one another as Christ loves us. Love is a Fruit of the Holy Spirit. Also, when someone tells us something we may not like, we must not react in agitation but we must practice self-control. Self-control is also a Fruit of the Holy Spirit.

But the fruit of the Spirit is: (1) charity/love; (2) joy; (3) peace; (4) patience; (5) kindness; (6) goodness; (7) faithfulness; (8) gentleness; and (9) self-control. Against such things there is no law. **Galatians 5:22-23.**

Each week, we will focus on a different topic. There will be daily readings and journal entries for these topics. **In Part I, we will read Galatians 5:22-23 DAILY along with the other daily reading(s).**

I pray this bible study is instrumental to each of us and help us grow to walk like Christ in our daily Christian walk.

Week 1: Charity/Love

Day 1 - _____

John 3:16 "For God so loved the world that He gave His only begotten Son, that whoever believes in Him should not perish but have everlasting life.";

Galatians 5:22-23 *"But the fruit of the Spirit is: (1) **charity/love**; (2) joy; (3) peace; (4) patience; (5) kindness; (6) goodness; (7) faithfulness; (8) gentleness; and (9) self-control. Against such things there is no law."*

Write about how grateful you are that God gave His one and only Son because He loved you so much.

_____

_____

_____

_____

Prayer: Lord, thank you for your unconditional love. Thank you for freely giving your one and only Son, Jesus Christ, to save a sinner like me. Lord, help me to love unconditionally as you love me unconditionally. In your darling Son, Jesus name. Amen.

Day 2 - _____

Romans 12:9 "Don't just pretend to love others. Really love them. Hate what is wrong. Hold tightly to what is good.";

Galatians 5:22-23 *"But the fruit of the Spirit is: (1) **charity/love**; (2) joy; (3) peace; (4) patience; (5) kindness; (6) goodness; (7) faithfulness; (8) gentleness; and (9) self-control. Against such things there is no law."*

Write about a time you loved someone else in a sincere manner, with no strings attached.

_____

_____

_____

_____

Prayer: Lord, help me to love others sincerely. Help me to love them without wanting anything in return from them. Help me to love others as you love me. Amen.

Day 3 - _____

Mark 12:31 "The second is equally important: 'Love your neighbor as yourself.'[a] No other commandment is greater than these.'"";

Romans 13:10 "Love does no wrong to others, so love fulfills the requirements of God's law.";

Galatians 5:22-23 *"But the fruit of the Spirit is: (1)* **charity/love**; *(2) joy; (3) peace; (4) patience; (5) kindness; (6) goodness; (7) faithfulness; (8) gentleness; and (9) self-control. Against such things there is no law."*

Write about how you can better love your neighbors. Your neighbor is any person who does not live in your own home. It can be a next-door neighbor, a church member, a co-worker, etc.

_____

_____

_____

_____

Prayer: Lord, help me to love my neighbors as I love myself. I pray that I love my neighbors unconditionally, despite how they may treat me. I know and understand that there is no greater commandment than to love my neighbors and I pray that I can love my neighbors as I love myself. Lord, give me the strength I need to fulfill this commandment so that you may show Your Mercy upon me. In your darling Son, Jesus name. Amen.

Day 4 - _____

1 Corinthians 13:4-8 "Love suffers long *and* is kind; love does not envy; love does not parade itself, is not puffed up; **5** does not behave rudely, does not seek its own, is not provoked, thinks no evil; **6** does not rejoice in iniquity, but rejoices in the truth; **7** bears all things, believes all things, hopes all things, endures all things. **8** Love never fails. But whether *there are* prophecies, they will fail; whether *there are* tongues, they will cease; whether *there is* knowledge, it will vanish away.";

Galatians 5:22-23 *"But the fruit of the Spirit is: (1)* **charity/love***; (2) joy; (3) peace; (4) patience; (5) kindness; (6) goodness; (7) faithfulness; (8) gentleness; and (9) self-control. Against such things there is no law."*

Write down your definition of love, giving synonyms. Also, write down what love is not, giving antonyms.

_____

_____

_____

_____

Prayer: Lord, help me to love and to be patient and kind. Help me to protect, trust, hope and persevere. Lord, help me to not envy or boast. Help me to not be rude, easily angered or self-seeking. Help me to not keep record of wrongs. Lord, help me to not delight in evil but help me to rejoice with the truth. In your darling Son, Jesus name. Amen.

Day 5 - _____

1 John 4:7-8 "Beloved, let us love one another, for love is of God; and everyone who loves is born of God and knows God. **8** He who does not love does not know God, for God is love.";

Galatians 5:22-23 *"But the fruit of the Spirit is: (1)* **charity/love***; (2) joy; (3) peace; (4) patience; (5) kindness; (6) goodness; (7) faithfulness; (8) gentleness; and (9) self-control. Against such things there is no law."*

Describe how God's Love helps you to love one another and testify how God's Love has helped you to love others.

_____

_____

_____

_____

Prayer: Lord, thank you for your Love. Thank you for your Grace and Mercy. Thank you for my family, friends, and neighbors. I pray that you help me to love others. I know and understand that to love others is to know you and he who does not love does not know you. I want to love others so others will know that I know You, Lord. You are love, God. In your darling Son, Jesus name. Amen.

<u>Day 6 - _____</u>

Proverbs 10:12 "Hatred stirs up strife, But love covers all sins.";
Galatians 5:22-23 *"But the fruit of the Spirit is: (1) **charity/love**; (2) joy; (3) peace; (4) patience; (5) kindness; (6) goodness; (7) faithfulness; (8) gentleness; and (9) self-control. Against such things there is no law."*

Write about a time hatred blocked you from loving God, yourself, and others. Describe how this made you feel and what you did to love again.

_____

_____

_____

_____

Prayer: Lord, thank you for this day. Thank you for teaching us how to love despite being hated. Lord, thank you for teaching me to love again when I once hated. Continue to teach me to love despite being hated and continue to teach me to love my neighbors and my enemies. In Jesus name. Amen.

<u>Day 7 - _____</u>

Luke 6:35 "But love your enemies, do good, and lend, hoping for nothing in return; and your reward will be great, and you will be sons of the Most High. For He is kind to the unthankful and evil.";
Galatians 5:22-23 *"But the fruit of the Spirit is: (1) **charity/love**; (2) joy; (3) peace; (4) patience; (5) kindness; (6) goodness; (7) faithfulness; (8) gentleness; and (9) self-control. Against such things there is no law."*

Write about a time where your "enemy" did something you did not like and you reacted out of love toward them. Or, write about a time

you should have acted in love toward an "enemy." Remembering that our one and only enemy is the devil; he just use people to do his work.

_____

_____

_____

_____

Prayer: Lord, thank you for this week's lesson on charity/love. Help me to love my enemies and to do good to them. Help me to treat them as I would want to be treated. Lord, help me to love them no matter how bad they may treat me. Lord, continue to love me so that I may love others and show Your Love to others so they will see You in me. In your darling Son, Jesus name I pray. Amen.

Don't let this paper go to waste. If there is something else you want to write about, relating to the subject of charity/love, then write it here!

Week 2: Joy

Day 8 - _____

Proverbs 10:28 "The aspirations of good people end in celebration; the ambitions of bad people crash.";

Galatians 5:22-23 *But the fruit of the Spirit is: (1) charity/love; (2)* ***joy****; (3) peace; (4) patience; (5) kindness; (6) goodness; (7) faithfulness; (8) gentleness; and (9) self-control. Against such things there is no law.*

What does this bible passage mean to you?

_____

_____

_____

_____

Prayer: Lord, thank you for this day. Thank you for week two of this bible study. Thank you for giving me joy, deep down in my soul. Lord, help me to continue to show love to my neighbors. When I am filled with sorrow, fill me with Your Joy. In Jesus name I pray. Amen.

Day 9 - _____

1 Peter 1:8-9 "whom having not seen[a] you love. Though now you do not see *Him,* yet believing, you rejoice with joy inexpressible and full of glory, **9** receiving the end of your faith—the salvation of *your* souls.";

Galatians 5:22-23 *But the fruit of the Spirit is: (1) charity/love; (2)* ***joy****; (3) peace; (4) patience; (5) kindness; (6) goodness; (7) faithfulness; (8) gentleness; and (9) self-control. Against such things there is no law.*

What/Who gives you joy? What/Who makes you joyful?

_____

_____

_____

_____

Prayer: Lord, I thank you for giving me joy. Although I've never seen You, I still have true joy in knowing You. Thank you for those blessings that also give me pure joy. But remind me that joy comes from You and no one or nothing else can give me the joy You give me. In Jesus name I pray. Amen.

Day 10 - _____

Hebrews 12:2 "looking unto Jesus, the author and finisher of *our* faith, who for the joy that was set before Him endured the cross, despising the shame, and has sat down at the right hand of the throne of God.";

Galatians 5:22-23 *But the fruit of the Spirit is: (1) charity/love; (2) **joy**; (3) peace; (4) patience; (5) kindness; (6) goodness; (7) faithfulness; (8) gentleness; and (9) self-control. Against such things there is no law.*

Write about the joy you feel knowing that God is the author and perfecter of your faith. How does your knowing this help you get through difficult times?

_____

_____

_____

_____

Prayer: Lord, thank you for being the author and perfecter of my faith. With this, I have great joy in my heart. Thank you for dying on the cross, paying the price for my sins. Lord, I love you and I praise you. I am thankful for the joy in my heart because I know it comes from You. I pray that I remember this in difficult times. In Jesus name I pray. Amen.

Day 11 - _____

James 1:2-4 "**2** My brethren, count it all joy when ye fall into divers temptations; **3** Knowing this, that the trying of your faith worketh patience. **4** But let patience have her perfect work, that ye may be perfect and entire, wanting nothing.";

Galatians 5:22-23 *But the fruit of the Spirit is: (1) charity/love; (2)* **joy***; (3) peace; (4) patience; (5) kindness; (6) goodness; (7) faithfulness; (8) gentleness; and (9) self-control. Against such things there is no law.*

Write about a time your faith was tested but you still had joy in your heart and soul. How did your reaction bless or minister to those around you?

_____

_____

_____

_____

Prayer: Lord, thank you for the tests, trials and tribulations in my life. And thank you for the good times in my life. Thank you that I can still count it all joy, no matter what the circumstances may be. Help me to be a beacon light to others that they can also count it all joy no matter what may be going on in their lives. In Jesus name. Amen.

Day 12 - _____

Jude 1:24-25 "**24** Now unto him that is able to keep you from falling, and to present you faultless before the presence of his glory with exceeding joy, **25** To the only wise God our Saviour, be glory and majesty, dominion and power, both now and ever. Amen.";

Galatians 5:22-23 *But the fruit of the Spirit is: (1) charity/love; (2)* **joy;** *(3) peace; (4) patience; (5) kindness; (6) goodness; (7) faithfulness; (8) gentleness; and (9) self-control. Against such things there is no law.*

Write about how having the Joy of The Lord keeps you from making bad decisions.

_____

_____

_____

_____

Prayer: Lord, thank you for keeping me from stumbling. Because I recognize You are the One who kept me from stumbling, I have great joy deep down in my soul. Thank you for making me feel blameless and still have joy when I do stumble and You pick me up. Lord, I thank you and I love you. It is in Jesus name I pray. Amen.

Day 13 - _____

Psalm 30:5 "For his anger endureth but a moment; in his favour is life: weeping may endure for a night, but joy cometh in the morning.";

Galatians 5:22-23 *But the fruit of the Spirit is: (1) charity/love; (2)* **joy;** *(3) peace; (4) patience; (5) kindness; (6) goodness; (7) faithfulness; (8) gentleness; and (9) self-control. Against such things there is no law.*

Write about a time you felt sorrowful and wept uncontrollably. Describe how it made you feel after a night of weeping. Then write how much joy you felt the next morning after prayer.

_____

_____

_____

_____

Prayer: Lord, I am so thankful that weeping may endure for a night but joy comes in the morning. No matter what happened today, I know that tomorrow is a new day with brand new grace, mercy and joy! Thank you Lord. I pray that I remember that weeping may endure for a night but joy does come in the morning. In Jesus name I pray. Amen.

Day 14 - _____

Philippians 4:4-5 "Rejoice in the Lord always. Again I will say, rejoice! **5** Let your gentleness be known to all men. The Lord *is* at hand.";

Galatians 5:22-23 *But the fruit of the Spirit is: (1) charity/love; (2)* **joy**; *(3) peace; (4) patience; (5) kindness; (6) goodness; (7) faithfulness; (8) gentleness; and (9) self-control. Against such things there is no law.*

Write down how you can always be full of joy or how you can turn a sorrowful situation into a joyful situation.

_____

_____

_____

_____

Prayer: Lord, thank you for this week's lesson on joy. I now know that joy comes from You and You alone, not people, things, or circumstances. Although people, things, and circumstances may make me happy, only You can give me joy. The world didn't give me this joy that I have and the world certainly cannot take it away from me. Thank you for the good times and the bad because I can still count it all joy because of You. Lord, thank you for letting me know that my weeping may endure for a night but joy comes in the morning. I love you and I praise you. In Jesus name I pray. Amen.

Don't let this paper go to waste. If there is something else you want to write about, relating to the subject of joy, then write it here!

Week 3: Peace

Day 15 - _____

Isaiah 48:17-19 "This is what the Lord says— your Redeemer, the Holy One of Israel: "I am the Lord your God, who teaches you what is good for you and leads you along the paths you should follow. **18** Oh, that you had listened to my commands! Then you would have had peace flowing like a gentle river and righteousness rolling over you like waves in the sea. **19** Your descendants would have been like the sands along the seashore— too many to count! There would have been no need for your destruction, or for cutting off your family name."";

Galatians 5:22-23 *But the fruit of the Spirit is: (1) charity/love; (2) joy; (3)* **peace***; (4) patience; (5) kindness; (6) goodness; (7) faithfulness; (8) gentleness; and (9) self-control. Against such things there is no law.*

In this passage, God spoke to the children of Israel. He told them that they would have peace like a river if they had kept His Commandments. Can you recall a time that you needed peace like a river (never ending) or could have used peace like a river but did not because you did not keep God's Commandments? Write that incident down and also write down how you can better keep God's Commandments so that you will have peace like a river (never ending).

_____

_____

_____

_____

Prayer: Lord, thank you for giving me peace. Help me to remain peaceful in hectic and stressful situations. Help me to remember to love and have joy and peace in my heart always. In Jesus name. Amen.

Day 16 - _____

John 16:33 "I have told you all this so that you may have peace in me. Here on earth you will have many trials and sorrows. But take heart, because I have overcome the world."";

Isaiah 26:3 "You will keep in perfect peace all who trust in you, all whose thoughts are fixed on you!";

2 Thessalonians 3:16 "Now may the Lord of peace himself give you his peace at all times and in every situation. The Lord be with you all.";

Galatians 5:22-23 *But the fruit of the Spirit is: (1) charity/love; (2) joy; (3) peace; (4) patience; (5) kindness; (6) goodness; (7) faithfulness; (8) gentleness; and (9) self-control. Against such things there is no law.*

Describe a time Jesus has given you peace when everything around you was giving you tribulation.

_____

_____

_____

_____

Prayer: Lord, thank you for Your Peace. Thank you for always being there with me and for me, especially during times of tribulations. I pray that I continue to walk in Your Peace. In Jesus name. Amen.

Day 17 - _____

Proverbs 16:7 "When a man's ways please the Lord, He makes even his enemies to be at peace with him.";

Galatians 5:22-23 *But the fruit of the Spirit is: (1) charity/love; (2) joy; (3) peace; (4) patience; (5) kindness; (6) goodness; (7) faithfulness; (8) gentleness; and (9) self-control. Against such things there is no law.*

Do you remember a time someone was upset with you but they could not show their true feelings but be at peace because of your walk with Christ? Describe that incident.

_____

_____

_____

_____

Prayer: Lord, thank you for making my enemies be at peace with me when they could hate and persecute me. Lord, thank you for Your Peace. Because of Your Peace, I also have peace and live a peaceful life, even against my enemies. Help me to continue to walk in Your Peace. In Jesus name. Amen.

Day 18 - _____

Psalm 120:6 "My soul has dwelt too long With one who hates peace.";
Galatians 5:22-23 *But the fruit of the Spirit is: (1) charity/love; (2) joy; (3) **peace**; (4) patience; (5) kindness; (6) goodness; (7) faithfulness; (8) gentleness; and (9) self-control. Against such things there is no law.*

Do you know someone who hates peace? How do you interact with them, if at all?

_____

_____

_____

_____

Prayer: Lord, help me to be at peace wherever I go. I pray for those who hate peace that they may come to know You and gain Your Peace. Help me to love those who hate peace. In Jesus name. Amen.

Day 19 - _____

Philippians 4:6-7 "Be anxious for nothing, but in everything by prayer and supplication, with thanksgiving, let your requests be made known to God; **7** and the peace of God, which surpasses all understanding, will guard your hearts and minds through Christ Jesus.";

Galatians 5:22-23 *But the fruit of the Spirit is: (1) charity/love; (2) joy; (3)* **peace***; (4) patience; (5) kindness; (6) goodness; (7) faithfulness; (8) gentleness; and (9) self-control. Against such things there is no law.*

How does prayer change the way you react to things? How does prayer give you the Peace of God?

_____

_____

_____

_____

Prayer: Lord, thank you for reminding me that I don't need to be anxious for anything because Your Peace will guard my heart and mind in Christ Jesus. I know I will receive Your Peace through prayer and petition so help me to pray more so I can receive Your Peace. In Jesus name. Amen.

Day 20 - _____

Psalm 34:14 "Depart from evil and do good; Seek peace and pursue it.";

Galatians 5:22-23 *But the fruit of the Spirit is: (1) charity/love; (2) joy; (3) **peace**; (4) patience; (5) kindness; (6) goodness; (7) faithfulness; (8) gentleness; and (9) self-control. Against such things there is no law.*

Have you ever sought peace? When and why?

_____

_____

_____

_____

Prayer: Lord, thank you for this day. Thank you for helping me to turn from evil to do good and to seek peace and pursue it. In Jesus name. Amen.

Day 21 - _____

John 14:27 "Peace I leave with you, My peace I give to you; not as the world gives do I give to you. Let not your heart be troubled, neither let it be afraid.";

Galatians 5:22-23 *But the fruit of the Spirit is: (1) charity/love; (2) joy; (3) **peace**; (4) patience; (5) kindness; (6) goodness; (7) faithfulness; (8) gentleness; and (9) self-control. Against such things there is no law.*

Describe God's Peace over your life. How does this influence your reactions to tribulations?

_____

_____

_____

_____

Prayer: Lord, thank you for this week's lesson on **peace**. Because of this lesson, I can now stand up straight in my tribulations and walk in Your Peace. I seek peace and pursue it. Thank you for letting me know that I can have peace because I have You. I do not have to be afraid and my heart will not be troubled because my peace is in You. Help me to remember these things in difficult times. In Jesus name. Amen.

Don't let this paper go to waste. If there is something else you want to write about, relating to the subject of peace, then write it here!

Week 4: Patience

Day 22 - _____

Romans 12:12 "rejoicing in hope, patient in tribulation, continuing steadfastly in prayer;";

Galatians 5:22-23 *But the fruit of the Spirit is: (1) charity/love; (2) joy; (3) peace; (4)* **patience***; (5) kindness; (6) goodness; (7) faithfulness; (8) gentleness; and (9) self-control. Against such things there is no law.*

How can you be patient in tribulations?

_____

_____

_____

_____

Prayer: Lord, thank you again for the first three weeks on love, joy and peace. Thank you for week four – patience. Lord, give me patience in all situations, even when I cannot see you working on my behalf. Give me the patience I need especially in tribulations. In Jesus name. Amen.

Day 23 - _____

Galatians 6:9 "And let us not grow weary while doing good, for in due season we shall reap if we do not lose heart.";

Galatians 5:22-23 *But the fruit of the Spirit is: (1) charity/love; (2) joy; (3) peace; (4)* **patience***; (5) kindness; (6) goodness; (7) faithfulness; (8) gentleness; and (9) self-control. Against such things there is no law.*

What is one thing you remained patient about receiving and God came through right on time? How did your patience at that time help you in future engagements where you needed to practice patience?

_____

_____

_____

_____

Prayer: Lord, again, I ask for patience. Help me to not give up. Help me to not grow weary of doing good. I know that in due season, I shall reap if I remain patient. In Jesus name. Amen.

Day 24 - _____

Isaiah 40:31 "But those who wait on the Lord Shall renew *their* strength; They shall mount up with wings like eagles, They shall run and not be weary, They shall walk and not faint.";
Galatians 5:22-23 *But the fruit of the Spirit is: (1) charity/love; (2) joy; (3) peace; (4) **patience**; (5) kindness; (6) goodness; (7) faithfulness; (8) gentleness; and (9) self-control. Against such things there is no law.*

What are you waiting for today? Ask God to give you the patience to wait on that thing or those things. Write your own prayer below.

_____

_____

_____

_____

Prayer: Write your own prayer asking God to give you patience to wait on that thing or those things you desire.

_____

_____

_____

_____

Day 25 - _____

Luke 8:15 "But the ones *that* fell on the good ground are those who, having heard the word with a noble and good heart, keep *it* and bear fruit with patience.";

James 5:7 "Therefore be patient, brethren, until the coming of the Lord. See *how* the farmer waits for the precious fruit of the earth, waiting patiently for it until it receives the early and latter rain.";

Galatians 5:22-23 *But the fruit of the Spirit is: (1) charity/love; (2) joy; (3) peace; (4)* **patience***; (5) kindness; (6) goodness; (7) faithfulness; (8) gentleness; and (9) self-control. Against such things there is no law.*

What seed have you planted that was reaped only when you practiced patience? In other words, what did you have to practice patience for in order to receive in your life?

_____

_____

_____

_____

Prayer: Lord, thank you for the seeds you have allowed me to plant. Moreover, thank you for giving me the patience to allow it to manifest.

Thank you for the reaping season. I pray that I continue to practice patience so that I may receive your blessings and promises for my life. Lord, continue to help me to practice patience. In Jesus name. Amen.

Day 26 -_____

2 Peter 1: 4-7 "**4** And because of his glory and excellence, he has given us great and precious promises. These are the promises that enable you to share his divine nature and escape the world's corruption caused by human desires. **5** In view of all this, make every effort to respond to God's promises. Supplement your faith with a generous provision of moral excellence, and moral excellence with knowledge, **6** and knowledge with self-control, and self-control with patient endurance, and patient endurance with godliness, **7** and godliness with brotherly affection, and brotherly affection with love for everyone.";

Galatians 5:22-23 *But the fruit of the Spirit is: (1) charity/love; (2) joy; (3) peace; (4)* **patience***; (5) kindness; (6) goodness; (7) faithfulness; (8) gentleness; and (9) self-control. Against such things there is no law.*

We have all heard the phrase "patience is a virtue." What does this mean to you?

_____

_____

_____

_____

Prayer: Lord, thank you again for Your Patience and help me to be patient. Because patience is a virtue, help me to practice patience so that I may be virtuous, giving You all the glory. In Jesus name. Amen.

Day 27 - _____

2 Peter 3:9 "The Lord isn't really being slow about his promise, as some people think. No, he is being patient for your sake. He does not want anyone to be destroyed, but wants everyone to repent.";

Galatians 5:22-23 *But the fruit of the Spirit is: (1) charity/love; (2) joy; (3) peace; (4)* **patience***; (5) kindness; (6) goodness; (7) faithfulness; (8) gentleness; and (9) self-control. Against such things there is no law.*

Write about a time God was patient with you.

_____

_____

_____

_____

Prayer: Lord, thank you for being so patient with me, even when I didn't deserve your patience. You waited for me so You can have me right where You want me, Lord and I thank You for that. Because you are patient with me, I can be patient with others. Lord, help me to be patient with others even when they press all of the wrong buttons. In Jesus name. Amen.

Day 28 - _____

1 Samuel 13:8-14 "**8** Then he waited seven days, according to the time set by Samuel. But Samuel did not come to Gilgal; and the people were scattered from him. **9** So Saul said, "Bring a burnt offering and peace offerings here to me." And he offered the burnt offering. **10** Now it happened, as soon as he had finished presenting the burnt offering, that Samuel came; and Saul went out to meet him, that he might greet him. **11** And Samuel said, "What have you done?" Saul said, "When I saw that the people were scattered from me, and *that* you did not come within the days appointed, and *that* the Philistines gathered together at Michmash, **12** then I said, 'The Philistines will now come down on me at Gilgal, and I have not made supplication to the Lord.' Therefore I felt compelled, and offered a burnt offering." **13** And Samuel said to Saul, "You have done foolishly. You have not kept the commandment of the Lord your God, which He commanded you. For now the Lord would have established your kingdom over Israel forever. **14** But now your kingdom shall not continue. The Lord has sought for Himself a man after His own heart, and the Lord has commanded him *to be* commander over His people, because you have not kept what the Lord commanded you."";

Galatians 5:22-23 *But the fruit of the Spirit is: (1) charity/love; (2) joy; (3) peace; (4)* **patience***; (5) kindness; (6) goodness; (7) faithfulness; (8) gentleness; and (9) self-control. Against such things there is no law.*

This passage describes when Saul lacked patience in waiting on The Lord. Because of this, Saul did not inherit the kingdom God had for him. Can you recall a time you did not inherit the kingdom God had for you because you lacked patience? Can you recall a time you gave up on something right before God was going to bless you?

_____

_____

_____

_____

Prayer: Lord, thank you for this week's lesson on patience. Continue to strengthen me and give me patience. Help me to be patient in times of tribulations. Help me to be patient with others just as You have been patient with me. Lord, I ask for Your Patience to get to the kingdom You have just for me. I ask all these things in Jesus name. Amen.

Week 5: Kindness

Day 29 - _____

Proverbs 3:3 "Let not mercy and truth forsake you; Bind them around your neck, Write them on the tablet of your heart,";

Galatians 5:22-23 *But the fruit of the Spirit is: (1) charity/love; (2) joy; (3) peace; (4) patience; (5) **kindness**; (6) goodness; (7) faithfulness; (8) gentleness; and (9) self-control. Against such things there is no law.*

How can you always show kindness?

_____

_____

_____

_____

Prayer: Lord, teach me and help me to be kind and truthful to others at all times. I pray that I practice kindness with my family, friends, and enemies. You were kind to everyone you came in contact with and I want to follow in Your footsteps. Help me, Lord, to be kind. In Jesus name. Amen.

Day 30 - _____

Micah 6:8 "He has shown you, O man, what *is* good; And what does the Lord require of you But to do justly, To love mercy, And to walk humbly with your God?";

Galatians 5:22-23 *But the fruit of the Spirit is: (1) charity/love; (2) joy; (3) peace; (4) patience; (5) **kindness**; (6) goodness; (7) faithfulness; (8) gentleness; and (9) self-control. Against such things there is no law.*

Other than to be kind to others, what else has God required you to do? Have you done it? If not, what is stopping you?

_____

_____

_____

_____

Prayer: Lord, thank you for requiring me to do justice and to love kindness. Lord, thank you also for your other requirements of me. I pray that I am fulfilling those requirements and if not, please place it on my heart to do so. In Jesus name. Amen.

Day 31 - _____

Hebrews 13:2 "Don't forget to show hospitality to strangers, for some who have done this have entertained angels without realizing it!";
Galatians 5:22-23 *But the fruit of the Spirit is: (1) charity/love; (2) joy; (3) peace; (4) patience; (5) **kindness**; (6) goodness; (7) faithfulness; (8) gentleness; and (9) self-control. Against such things there is no law.*

Describe a time you were kind to complete strangers. Was your kindness accepted or rejected?

_____

_____

_____

_____

Prayer: Lord, help me to be kind to strangers as You were. If my kindness is not accepted or appreciated, please help me to continue to be kind to strangers. Don't allow others' reactions and perceptions stop me from fulfilling Your good work. In Jesus name. Amen.

Day 32 - _____

Acts 28:2 "The people of the island were very kind to us. It was cold and rainy, so they built a fire on the shore to welcome us.";

Galatians 5:22-23 *But the fruit of the Spirit is: (1) charity/love; (2) joy; (3) peace; (4) patience; (5) **kindness**; (6) goodness; (7) faithfulness; (8) gentleness; and (9) self-control. Against such things there is no law.*

Remember, after Hurricane Katrina how so many people across the nation showed acts of kindness to New Orleanians? If you have this type of encounter, please describe. It does not have to be during Hurricane Katrina.

_____

_____

_____

_____

Prayer: Lord, help me to be kind to those in great need. Help me to recognize "needs" versus "wants" and help those who truly need the help. Lord, I pray that my kindness is not taken as a weakness and in the event that it is, that I will not be discouraged to help others in their time of need. In Jesus name I pray. Amen.

Day 33 - _____

Genesis 20:13 " When God called me to leave my father's home and to travel from place to place, I told her, 'Do me a favor. Wherever we go, tell the people that I am your brother.'";

Galatians 5:22-23 *But the fruit of the Spirit is: (1) charity/love; (2) joy; (3) peace; (4) patience; (5)* **kindness***; (6) goodness; (7) faithfulness; (8) gentleness; and (9) self-control. Against such things there is no law.*

How do you show kindness to others?

_____

_____

_____

_____

Prayer: Lord, help me to never be a stranger to anyone that I meet. Help me to be kind to all I come in contact with. In Jesus name. Amen.

Day 34 - _____

1 Samuel 20:14-15 "**14** And you shall not only show me the kindness of the Lord while I still live, that I may not die; **15** but you shall not cut off your kindness from my house forever, no, not when the Lord has cut off every one of the enemies of David from the face of the earth.'''';

Galatians 5:22-23 *But the fruit of the Spirit is: (1) charity/love; (2) joy; (3) peace; (4) patience; (5)* **kindness***; (6) goodness; (7) faithfulness; (8) gentleness; and (9) self-control. Against such things there is no law.*

What is unfailing kindness? How can we show unfailing kindness?

_____

_____

_____

_____

Prayer: Lord, thank you for Your Unfailing Kindness. Because of Your Unfailing Kindness, I also can show unfailing kindness to those around me. Help me to show unfailing kindness to others so that they may see You in me and want to know You. In Jesus name. Amen.

Day 35 - _____

2 Samuel 2:5-6 "**5** So David sent messengers to the men of Jabesh Gilead, and said to them, "You *are* blessed of the Lord, for you have shown this kindness to your lord, to Saul, and have buried him. **6** And now may the Lord show kindness and truth to you. I also will repay you this kindness, because you have done this thing.";

Galatians 5:22-23 *But the fruit of the Spirit is: (1) charity/love; (2) joy; (3) peace; (4) patience; (5)* **kindness***; (6) goodness; (7) faithfulness; (8) gentleness; and (9) self-control. Against such things there is no law.*

What has The Lord blessed you with just for being kind to others?

_____

_____

_____

_____   _____

Prayer: Lord, thank you for this week's lesson on **kindness**. Thank you for your loving kindness and your unfailing kindness. Thank you for requiring me to be kind to others, especially strangers. Lord, help me to be kind to all that I come in contact with, including strangers. And by doing this, may I be blessed with the same unfailing kindness You have. Help me to always sow loving kindness and unfailing to kindness to all I may come in contact with. In Jesus name I pray. Amen.

Week 6: Goodness

Day 36 - _____

Romans 8:28 "And we know that all things work together for good to those who love God, to those who are the called according to *His* purpose.";

Galatians 5:22-23 *But the fruit of the Spirit is: (1) charity/love; (2) joy; (3) peace; (4) patience; (5) kindness; (6) **goodness**; (7) faithfulness; (8) gentleness; and (9) self-control. Against such things there is no law.*

Write down a time God showed goodness toward you because of your relationship with Him.

_____

_____

_____

_____

Prayer: Lord, thank you for last week's lesson on kindness. Help me to continue to be kind to others. Lord, thank you for this week's lesson on goodness. Thank you for Your Goodness. Thank you for working things out for my good even when I cannot see it at the time. I know that all things will work out for my good because I love you, Lord and because I am called to Your Purpose. Thank you and I love you. In Jesus name. Amen.

Day 37 - _____

Psalm 23:6 "Surely goodness and mercy shall follow me all the days of my life; And I will dwell[a] in the house of the Lord Forever.";

Galatians 5:22-23 *But the fruit of the Spirit is: (1) charity/love; (2) joy; (3) peace; (4) patience; (5) kindness; (6) **goodness**; (7) faithfulness; (8) gentleness; and (9) self-control. Against such things there is no law.*

Poem: "Mrs. Shirley Goodnest"

Timmy was a little five-year-old boy that his Mom loved very much and, being a worrier, she was concerned about him walking to school all by himself when he started kindergarten. She walked him to school the first few days, but one day he came home and asked if he could walk by himself. He wanted to be like the "big boys."

Not wanting to disappoint him, she decided to allow him to walk without her, via plan B (which consisted of recruiting a neighbor, Mrs. Goodnest, to repetitiously follow him to school, at a distance far enough behind him that he would not likely notice he was being followed, but close enough to keep a watch on him).

Mrs. Goodnest was agreeable, since she was up early with her own toddler anyway, and it would be a good way for them to get some exercise. So, the very next school day Mrs. Goodnest and her little girl, Marcy, set out to follow behind Timmy as he walked to school. Timmy was accompanied by another neighbor boy he knew.

As the boys walked to school each day, chatting, and kicking stones and twigs, the little friend of Timmy began to notice that a lady seemed to be following them every day.

"Have you noticed that lady following us all week? Do you know her?" he asked Timmy.

"Yea, I know who she is," Timmy replied.

"Well who is she?"

"That's just Shirley Goodnest," Timmy said.

"Shirley Goodnest? Who the is she? Why is she following us?"

"Well," Timmy explained, "Every night Mom makes me say the 23rd Psalm in my prayers 'cuz she worries about me so much. And in it the Psalm says, 'Shirley Goodnest and Marcy shall follow me all the days of my life,' so I guess I'll just have to get used to it."

Prayer: Lord, thank you for my own Mrs. Shirley Goodnest. Thank you for the poem that reminded me that SURELY, GOODNESS and lovingkindness shall follow me all the days of my life. Help me to remember this when I feel like I am walking all alone. In Jesus name I do pray. Amen.

Day 38 - _____

Psalm 34:8 "Oh, taste and see that the Lord *is* good; Blessed *is* the man *who* trusts in Him!";

Galatians 5:22-23 *But the fruit of the Spirit is: (1) charity/love; (2) joy; (3) peace; (4) patience; (5) kindness; (6)* **goodness***; (7) faithfulness; (8) gentleness; and (9) self-control. Against such things there is no law.*

When did you get a "taste" of God's goodness? Describe here.

_____

_____

_____

_____

Prayer: Lord, thank you again for Your Goodness! Thank you for giving me a "taste" of Your Goodness. I now yearn for more. Lord, please continue to be good to me and I promise to remain faithful to you. In Jesus name Amen.

Day 39 - _____

1 Timothy 6:18 "*Let them* do good, that they be rich in good works, ready to give, willing to share,";

But the fruit of the Spirit is: (1) charity/love; (2) joy; (3) peace;

Galatians 5:22-23 *But the fruit of the Spirit is: (1) charity/love; (2) joy;*

*(3) peace; (4) patience; (5) kindness; (6) **goodness**; (7) faithfulness; (8) gentleness; and (9) self-control. Against such things there is no law.*

How can you be rich in good works to others?

_____

_____

_____

_____

Prayer: Lord, help me to be rich in good works. Help me to do good and not expect anything in return. I know that you love cheerful givers so help me to give cheerfully. And, Lord, I pray that those who receive good works from me will also do good works for others. In Jesus name. Amen.

Day 40 - _____

Ephesians 6:7 "with goodwill doing service, as to the Lord, and not to men,";
Galatians 5:22-23 *But the fruit of the Spirit is: (1) charity/love; (2) joy; (3) peace; (4) patience; (5) kindness; (6) **goodness**; (7) faithfulness; (8) gentleness; and (9) self-control. Against such things there is no law.*

Do you do good works for God or for man? Whom do you expect a "job well done" from?

_____

_____

_____

_____

Prayer: Lord, thank you for reminding me that my good works are not in vain when done for Your Glory. I ask for forgiveness for times I have done good works for man's approval and I ask that You help me to do good works for Your Glory. In Jesus name. Amen.

Day 41 - _____
1 Chronicles 16:34 "Oh, give thanks to the Lord, for *He is* good! For His mercy *endures* forever.";
Galatians 5:22-23 *But the fruit of the Spirit is: (1) charity/love; (2) joy; (3) peace; (4) patience; (5) kindness; (6)* **goodness***; (7) faithfulness; (8) gentleness; and (9) self-control. Against such things there is no law.*

I know there are many things you will be able to think of to write down but write down ONE GOOD thing that you are thankful to God for.

_____

_____

_____

_____

Prayer: Lord, I give you thanks for everything you have done in my life: the good, the bad, and the ugly. I especially thank you for all of the good things you have done for me. And when they are not so good, help me to see the good in all situations. In Jesus name. Amen.

Day 42 - _____
Psalm 31:19-20 "**19** Oh, how great *is* Your goodness, Which You have laid up for those who fear You, *Which* You have prepared for those who trust in You In the presence of the sons of men! **20** You shall hide them in the secret place of Your presence From the plots of man; You

shall keep them secretly in a pavilion From the strife of tongues.";

Galatians 5:22-23 *But the fruit of the Spirit is: (1) charity/love; (2) joy; (3) peace; (4) patience; (5) kindness; (6)* **goodness***; (7) faithfulness; (8) gentleness; and (9) self-control. Against such things there is no law.*

Describe how you have felt a difference in God's Goodness toward you since giving your life to Him (if you have noticed a difference).

_____

_____

_____

_____

Prayer: Lord, thank you for this week's lesson on **goodness**. I thank you for Your Goodness and I ask that You help me to be good to others as You are so good to me. I pray that my good works are not in vain in Your Sight and that I do good works for Your Glory and not man's approval. Help me to keep my mind on You, Lord. In Jesus name. Amen.

Don't let this paper go to waste. If there is something else you want to write about, relating to the subject of goodness, then write it here!

Week 7: Faithfulness

Day 43 - _____

Deuteronomy 7:9 "Therefore know that the Lord your God, He *is* God, the faithful God who keeps covenant and mercy for a thousand generations with those who love Him and keep His commandments;";

Galatians 5:22-23 *But the fruit of the Spirit is: (1) charity/love; (2) joy; (3) peace; (4) patience; (5) kindness; (6) goodness; (7)* **faithfulness**; *(8) gentleness; and (9) self-control. Against such things there is no law.*

We know that God is faithful, but how faithful are you to God? How can you improve in your faithfulness to God?

_____

_____

_____

_____

Prayer: Lord, thank you for Your Faithfulness you show me every single day. Thank you for never giving up on me even when I wanted to give up on myself. Thank you for Your Commandments and I pray that I keep Your Commandments to show my faithfulness to you. In Jesus name. Amen.

Day 44 - _____

1 Corinthians 10:13 " No temptation has overtaken you except such as is common to man; but God *is* faithful, who will not allow you to be tempted beyond what you are able, but with the temptation will also make the way of escape, that you may be able to bear *it.* ";

2 Thessalonians 3:3 "But the Lord is faithful, who will establish you and guard *you* from the evil one.";

Galatians 5:22-23 *But the fruit of the Spirit is: (1) charity/love; (2) joy; (3) peace; (4) patience; (5) kindness; (6) goodness; (7)* **faithfulness***; (8) gentleness; and (9) self-control. Against such things there is no law.*

When has God guarded you from "evil" and you remained faithful to God?

_____

_____

_____

_____

Prayer: Lord, please guard me from all evil and help me to remain faithful to you. Lord, help me to never go astray from you. Lord, I pray that I remember Your Faithfulness when I am tempted to do evil and remain faithful to You. In Jesus name. Amen.

Day 45 - _____

Proverbs 28:20 "A faithful man will abound with blessings, But he who hastens to be rich will not go unpunished.";

Galatians 5:22-23 *But the fruit of the Spirit is: (1) charity/love; (2) joy; (3) peace; (4) patience; (5) kindness; (6) goodness; (7)* **faithfulness***; (8) gentleness; and (9) self-control. Against such things there is no law.*

What does this bible passage mean to you?

_____

_____

_____

_____

Prayer: Lord, help me to remain faithful to the things You have blessed me with. Help me to not abandon those things You have blessed me with to make a quick "come-up". In Jesus name. Amen.

Day 46 - _____

Luke 16:10-12 "**10** "If you are faithful in little things, you will be faithful in large ones. But if you are dishonest in little things, you won't be honest with greater responsibilities. **11** And if you are untrustworthy about worldly wealth, who will trust you with the true riches of heaven? **12** And if you are not faithful with other people's things, why should you be trusted with things of your own?";

Galatians 5:22-23 *But the fruit of the Spirit is: (1) charity/love; (2) joy; (3) peace; (4) patience; (5) kindness; (6) goodness; (7) **faithfulness**; (8) gentleness; and (9) self-control. Against such things there is no law.*

What "few things" have you been faithful over and God has rewarded you with much for your faithfulness?

_____

_____

_____

_____

Prayer: Lord, thank you for rewarding me for my faithfulness over few things. I am grateful to You for Your Faithfulness. I pray that others see and recognize Your Faithfulness and rewarding those who are faithful over few things. Lord, help me to be faithful over few things. In Jesus name. Amen.

Day 47 - _____

Ezekiel 18:9 "and faithfully obeys my decrees and regulations. Anyone who does these things is just and will surely live, says the Sovereign Lord.";

Galatians 5:22-23 *But the fruit of the Spirit is: (1) charity/love; (2) joy; (3) peace; (4) patience; (5) kindness; (6) goodness; (7) **faithfulness**; (8) gentleness; and (9) self-control. Against such things there is no law.*

How has your faithfulness kept you close to God? Or how did your lack of faithfulness keep you away from God?

_____

_____

_____

_____

Prayer: Lord, I thank you for keeping me safe and I pray that I remain faithful to You. No matter what is going on around me, I know that I can call on You and You will be there because You are faithful. I pray that I am as faithful to You as You are to me. When I am not, help me to get back on track. In Jesus name. Amen.

Day 48 - _____

1 Corinthians 15:58 "Therefore, my beloved brethren, be steadfast, immovable, always abounding in the work of the Lord, knowing that your labor is not in vain in the Lord.";

Galatians 5:22-23 *But the fruit of the Spirit is: (1) charity/love; (2) joy; (3) peace; (4) patience; (5) kindness; (6) goodness; (7) **faithfulness**; (8) gentleness; and (9) self-control. Against such things there is no law.*

How well does this verse describe your faithfulness to God? To others? To things?

_____

_____

_____

_____

Prayer: Lord, help me to be as faithful to You as I am to my family, friends, church and career. Help me to be steadfast, unmovable, and always abounding in Your Work. Remind me that my labor is not in vain when done for You and Your Glory. Help me to remain faithful to You. In Jesus name. Amen.

Day 49 - _____

Hebrews 13:8 "Jesus Christ *is* the same yesterday, today, and forever.";

Galatians 5:22-23 *But the fruit of the Spirit is: (1) charity/love; (2) joy; (3) peace; (4) patience; (5) kindness; (6) goodness; (7) **faithfulness**; (8) gentleness; and (9) self-control. Against such things there is no law.*

How amazing is God's faithfulness to You? Who is as faithful to you as God is?

_____

_____

_____

_____

Prayer: Lord, thank you so much for this week's lesson on **faithfulness**. This week's lesson has taught me so much about You and myself that I did not know before. I learned that Your Faithfulness is forever and it is the same today as it was yesterday and will be tomorrow and forever more. Lord, help me to be more faithful to you in my daily walk. Help me to be more faithful to You than I am to myself, my family, my friends, my church, and my career. Thank You for rewarding me for my faithfulness over few things, Lord. And help others see Your Faithfulness so they may draw nearer to You. In Jesus name. Amen.

Don't let this paper go to waste. If there is something else you want to write about, relating to the subject of faithfulness, then write it here!

Week 8: Gentleness

Day 50 - _____

Proverbs 15:1 "A soft answer turns away wrath, But a harsh word stirs up anger.";

Galatians 5:22-23 *But the fruit of the Spirit is: (1) charity/love; (2) joy; (3) peace; (4) patience; (5) kindness; (6) goodness; (7) faithfulness; (8)* **gentleness***; and (9) self-control. Against such things there is no law.*

When has your gentle speech calmed a situation? When has your harsh words irritated a situation?

_____

_____

_____

_____

Prayer: Lord, help me to answer gently so that there is no confusion and no wrath. Lord, help me to not use harsh words to avoid stirring up anger. Lord, give me the words to use so that I am gentle in my speech and not stirring up anger. In Jesus name. Amen.

Day 51 - _____

Colossians 4:5-6 "**5** Walk in wisdom toward those *who are* outside, redeeming the time. **6** *Let* your speech always *be* with grace, seasoned with salt, that you may know how you ought to answer each one.";

Galatians 5:22-23 *But the fruit of the Spirit is: (1) charity/love; (2) joy; (3) peace; (4) patience; (5) kindness; (6) goodness; (7) faithfulness; (8)* **gentleness***; and (9) self-control. Against such things there is no law.*

Is your speech/voice gentle? How can you speak more gently?

_____

_____

_____

_____

Prayer: Lord, touch my lips and my tongue that I may speak with grace and with gentleness so that Your Grace and Your Gentleness may show. In Jesus name. Amen.

Day 52 - _____

Titus 3:1-2 "Remind them to be subject to rulers and authorities, to obey, to be ready for every good work, **2** to speak evil of no one, to be peaceable, gentle, showing all humility to all men.";

Galatians 5:22-23 *But the fruit of the Spirit is: (1) charity/love; (2) joy; (3) peace; (4) patience; (5) kindness; (6) goodness; (7) faithfulness; (8) **gentleness**; and (9) self-control. Against such things there is no law.*

Writing: Write this bible verse (Titus 3:2) four times.

_____

_____

_____

_____

_____

_____

_____

_____

_____

_____

_____

_____

Prayer: Lord, help me to be gentle to all I come in contact with. Help me to not speak evil of no man. Show me how to be gentle and meek and mild-tempered. When I want to speak evil of another, Lord, please shut my mouth. When I want to fight, tie my hands. Encourage me to be gentile and meek to all men. It is in Jesus name I do pray. Amen.

Day 53 - _____

Galatians 6:1 "Brethren, if a man is overtaken in any trespass, you who *are* spiritual restore such a one in a spirit of gentleness, considering yourself lest you also be tempted.";

Galatians 5:22-23 *But the fruit of the Spirit is: (1) charity/love; (2) joy; (3) peace; (4) patience; (5) kindness; (6) goodness; (7) faithfulness; (8)* **gentleness***; and (9) self-control. Against such things there is no law.*

When/how has your gentle spirit been tempted?

_____

_____

_____

_____

Prayer: Lord, help me to remain gentle at all times, and not be tempted by the evil ways of the world. When I am tempted to not be gentle, help me to remember that gentleness is Christ-like. In Jesus name. Amen.

Day 54 - _____

1 Timothy 6:10-11 "**10** For the love of money is a root of all *kinds of* evil, for which some have strayed from the faith in their greediness, and pierced themselves through with many sorrows. **11** But you, O man of God, flee these things and pursue righteousness, godliness, faith, love, patience, gentleness.";

Galatians 5:22-23 *But the fruit of the Spirit is: (1) charity/love; (2) joy; (3) peace; (4) patience; (5) kindness; (6) goodness; (7) faithfulness; (8)* **gentleness**; *and (9) self-control. Against such things there is no law.*

How has this verse been taken out of context? What does this verse really mean?

_____

_____

_____

_____

Prayer: Lord, help me to pursue righteousness, Godliness, faith, love, patience and gentleness. Help me to flee from those things that are not of God. In Jesus name. Amen.

Day 55 - _____

Matthew 11:25-30 "**25** At that time Jesus prayed this prayer: "O Father, Lord of heaven and earth, thank you for hiding these things from those who think themselves wise and clever, and for revealing them to the childlike. **26** Yes, Father, it pleased you to do it this way!

27 "My Father has entrusted everything to me. No one truly knows the Son except the Father, and no one truly knows the Father except the Son and those to whom the Son chooses to reveal him." **28** Then Jesus said, "Come to me, all of you who are weary and carry heavy burdens, and I will give you rest. **29** Take my yoke upon you. Let me teach you, because I am humble and gentle at heart, and you will find rest for your souls. **30** For my yoke is easy to bear, and the burden I give you is light.""";

Galatians 5:22-23 *But the fruit of the Spirit is: (1) charity/love; (2) joy; (3) peace; (4) patience; (5) kindness; (6) goodness; (7) faithfulness; (8) **gentleness**; and (9) self-control. Against such things there is no law.*

In what ways has God been gentle with you? Do you think you deserve His Gentleness?

_____

_____

_____

_____

Prayer: Lord, thank you for Your Gentleness toward me even when I may not have deserved it. Thank you for giving me rest and taking my burdens. I pray that I follow you all the days of my life. In Jesus name I pray. Amen.

Day 56 - _____

Philippians 4:5 "Let your gentleness be known to all men. The Lord *is* at hand.";

Galatians 5:22-23 *But the fruit of the Spirit is: (1) charity/love; (2) joy; (3) peace; (4) patience; (5) kindness; (6) goodness; (7) faithfulness; (8) **gentleness**; and (9) self-control. Against such things there is no law.*

Do people perceive you to be gentle? If not, how can you change your ways so that you are known to be gentle to those around you?

_____

_____

_____

_____

Prayer: Lord, thank you for this week's lesson on **gentleness**. I pray that my speech and actions are gentle and when they are not, that you remind me to be gentle to all I come in contact with. Lord, thank you for Your Gentleness toward me even when I did not deserve it. Help me to pursue righteousness, Godliness, faith, love, patience and gentleness. Help me to flee from those things that are not of God. In Jesus name. Amen.

Don't let this paper go to waste. If there is something else you want to write about, relating to the subject of gentleness, then write it here!

Week 9: Self-Control

Day 57 - _____

Psalm 141:3 "Set a guard, O Lord, over my mouth; Keep watch over the door of my lips.";

Galatians 5:22-23 *But the fruit of the Spirit is: (1) charity/love; (2) joy; (3) peace; (4) patience; (5) kindness; (6) goodness; (7) faithfulness; (8) gentleness; and (9)* **self-control***. Against such things there is no law.*

How much self-control do you have over your tongue/words? How can you gain more self-control in that area?

_____

_____

_____

_____

Prayer: Lord, help me to practice self-control in all areas of my life, but specifically over my mouth. Help me to speak good and not bad. Help me to speak positive and not negative. Help me to speak with gentleness. In Jesus name. Amen.

Day 58 - _____

1 Peter 5:8 "Be sober, be vigilant; because[a] your adversary the devil walks about like a roaring lion, seeking whom he may devour.";

Galatians 5:22-23 *But the fruit of the Spirit is: (1) charity/love; (2) joy; (3) peace; (4) patience; (5) kindness; (6) goodness; (7) faithfulness; (8) gentleness; and (9)* **self-control***. Against such things there is no law.*

How much self-control do you have over your actions? How can you gain more self-control in that area?

_____

_____

_____

_____

Prayer: Lord, help me to practice self-control in all areas of my life, but specifically over my actions. Help me to do Your Work and that my light will shine for You. Help me to do good and not evil because I know the devil is on my heels. Help me to stay grounded in Your Word because my adversary is waiting for me to mess up. In Jesus name. Amen.

Day 59 - _____

1 Thessalonians 5:6-8 "**6** Therefore let us not sleep, as others *do,* but let us watch and be sober. **7** For those who sleep, sleep at night, and those who get drunk are drunk at night. **8** But let us who are of the day be sober, putting on the breastplate of faith and love, and *as* a helmet the hope of salvation.";

Galatians 5:22-23 *But the fruit of the Spirit is: (1) charity/love; (2) joy; (3) peace; (4) patience; (5) kindness; (6) goodness; (7) faithfulness; (8) gentleness; and (9)* **self-control***. Against such things there is no law.*

Are you easily influenced by others or do you have much self-control?

_____

_____

_____

_____

Prayer: Lord, help me to be watchful and cautious of those who may try to get me off of track and away from You and Your Word. Help me to remain sober and vigilant. In Jesus name. Amen.

Day 60 - _____

Proverbs 29:11 "A fool vents all his feelings,[a] But a wise *man* holds them back.";

Galatians 5:22-23 *But the fruit of the Spirit is: (1) charity/love; (2) joy; (3) peace; (4) patience; (5) kindness; (6) goodness; (7) faithfulness; (8) gentleness; and (9)* **self-control**. *Against such things there is no law.*

How much self-control do you have when you are angry or upset?

_____

_____

_____

_____

Prayer: Lord, help me to practice self-control at all times, even when I am angry or upset. Help me to be wise and hold my tongue when I am angry or upset. In Jesus name. Amen.

Day 61 - _____

1 Corinthians 10:13 "No temptation has overtaken you except such as is common to man; but God *is* faithful, who will not allow you to be tempted beyond what you are able, but with the temptation will also make the way of escape, that you may be able to bear *it.*";

Galatians 5:22-23 *But the fruit of the Spirit is: (1) charity/love; (2) joy; (3) peace; (4) patience; (5) kindness; (6) goodness; (7) faithfulness; (8) gentleness; and (9)* **self-control**. *Against such things there is no law.*

Ask God to give you self-control so that no temptation will overtake you.

_____

_____

_____

_____

Prayer: Lord, thank you for Your Faithfulness. Thank you for giving me self-control when I could have been tempted by my adversary. Thank you for not allowing me to be tempted beyond my ability. You know all about me all the way to the number of hairs on my head and you know just how much I can handle. Thank you Lord. In Jesus name. Amen.

Day 62 - _____

Titus 2:1-8 "**1-6** Your job is to speak out on the things that make for solid doctrine. Guide older men into lives of temperance, dignity, and wisdom, into healthy faith, love, and endurance. Guide older women into lives of reverence so they end up as neither gossips nor drunks, but models of goodness. By looking at them, the younger women will know how to love their husbands and children, be virtuous and pure, keep a good house, be good wives. We don't want anyone looking down on God's Message because of their behavior. Also, guide the young men to live disciplined lives. **7-8** But mostly, show them all this by doing it yourself, incorruptible in your teaching, your words solid and sane. Then anyone who is dead set against us, when he finds nothing weird or misguided, might eventually come around.";

Galatians 5:22-23 *But the fruit of the Spirit is: (1) charity/love; (2) joy; (3) peace; (4) patience; (5) kindness; (6) goodness; (7) faithfulness; (8) gentleness; and (9)* **self-control***. Against such things there is no law.*

What does being older have to do with having self-control? If you do not have self-control, how can you gain self-control?

_____

_____

_____

_____

Prayer: Lord, thank you for another day in Your Glory. Thank you for letting me make it this far. I pray that you continue to lead me and guide me. Lord, help me to control my own words, thoughts and actions that are pleasing to You. Give me self-control, especially in times that are the most difficult to practice self-control. In Jesus name. Amen.

Day 63 - _____

1 Peter 4:7 "The end of the world is coming soon. Therefore, be earnest and disciplined in your prayers.";

Galatians 5:22-23 *But the fruit of the Spirit is: (1) charity/love; (2) joy; (3) peace; (4) patience; (5) kindness; (6) goodness; (7) faithfulness; (8) gentleness; and (9)* **self-control***. Against such things there is no law.*

How does a prayer life help us with having self-control?

_____

_____

_____

_____

Prayer: Lord, thank you for this week's lesson in **self-control**. Help us to have self-control always, even when we become angry or upset and when our adversary tries to tempt us. Help us to practice self-control over our words and actions so that they are Christ-like and that You are glorified. When we are tempted, help us remember that You are faithful and will never allow us to be tempted beyond our ability. In Jesus name. Amen.

Don't let this paper go to waste. If there is something else you want to write about, relating to the subject of self-control, then write it here!

Part II – The Armor of God

Part II will be more of a weekly bible lesson. Instead of having daily readings, we will read as much or as little in a day, trying to finish each section before the next week's lesson.

Each week will bring on a new song that will be listed at the beginning of the week's lesson. Listen to the song each day that week to help you stand against the devil.

In Part II, we will dissect the Armor of God. There are seven pieces to the Armor of God: (1) belt of truth; (2) breastplate of righteousness; (3) shoes of peace; (4) shield of faith; (5) helmet of salvation; (6) sword of the Spirit; and (7) PRAYER.

We are instructed to "PUT ON" the whole armor of God, which implies that we do not automatically wear it all the time. Putting on the Armor of God requires a conscious decision on our part. It also requires effort from each of us.

During Part II of this bible study, we will work on the most important part of the Armor of God – PRAYER! Prayer is the most important piece because it is our way of communicating with God. How can we say we have a relationship with someone and we don't even talk to them? So, during this time, I want you to pray without ceasing. PRAY PRAY PRAY! While you are praying for your own situation(s), remember to pray for others.

The song we will listen to each day is: "Victory" by Yolanda Adams which can be listened to on YouTube. Just search "Victory by Yolanda Adams." Do the same for the weekly songs as well.

Please listen to the song daily to remind yourself that you do, indeed, have the VICTORY in Christ Jesus. Why put on the Armor of God and not be Victorious???

Week 10: Belt of Truth and Breastplate of Righteousness

Days 64 – 70 - _____
Songs: **"Take Away" by Yolanda Adams**

"Victory" by Yolanda Adams

Ephesians 6:10-18
*10 Finally, be strong in the Lord and in his mighty power. 11 Put on the full armor of God, so that you can take your stand against the devil's schemes. 12 For our struggle is not against flesh and blood, but against the rulers, against the authorities, against the powers of this dark world and against the spiritual forces of evil in the heavenly realms. 13 Therefore put on the full armor of God, so that when the day of evil comes, you may be able to stand your ground, and after you have done everything, to stand. **14 Stand firm then, with the belt of truth buckled around your waist, with the breastplate of righteousness in place,** 15 and with your feet fitted with the readiness that comes from the gospel of peace. 16 In addition to all this, take up the shield of faith, with which you can extinguish all the flaming arrows of the evil one. 17 Take the helmet of salvation and the sword of the Spirit, which is the word of God. 18 And pray in the Spirit on all occasions with all kinds of prayers and requests. With this in mind, be alert and always keep on praying for all the Lord's people.* **Ephesians 6:10-18.**

BELT OF TRUTH – THE TRUTH, THE WHOLE TRUTH, AND NOTHING BUT THE TRUTH

In the Roman army, the belt played a crucial role in the effectiveness of a soldier's armor. It was the belt that held the scabbard, without which there would be no place to put a sword. From the belt hung strips of leather to protect the lower body. The belt "girds on" or secures all of the other pieces of the armor. The belt kept the soldier's clothing from flapping about and allowed the soldier freedom of movement. The belt was also used to strengthen and support the body and it helped hold the breastplate in place. Therefore, truth should cleave to us as a belt cleaves to our body.

Truth is essential to our existence. We base our decisions on what we know, and if what we know is not the truth, we will make very bad decisions. For example, the gas gauge must tell us the truth so that we do not run out of gas. We want the truth from our spouses or significant others so that our marriage/relationship can be all that it is meant to be.

So, what exactly is the belt of truth? First, Christ is the truth and we, as believers, are to "put on" Christ. When we gave our lives to Christ, we were renewed, or born again. *2 Cor. 5:17* says, "Therefore if any man be in Christ, he is a new creature: old things are passed away; behold, all things are become new." We have become spiritually minded. He is a new man, created by Christ and has been given a holy nature and an incorruptible life. He is a man who is (1) in fellowship with God, (2) obedient to God's Will, and (3) devoted to God's Service. Every person can have a new beginning, a new life by coming to Jesus Christ ONLY by the Power of God!

Second, the Word of God is truth. We, as Christians, must put on the Word of God. Without the Word of God, how can we fight off the enemy? The Word of God said to resist the devil and he will flee from you (*James 4:7*). One way we can resist the devil is to "put on" the Word of God. Putting on the Word of God means to read our Bibles and hide it in our hearts so that we will not sin against God (*Psalm 119:11*).

To be girded with truth is to be firmly established in the truth of God's Word. Just as the soldier's belt provided freedom of movement, we are kept FREE from the enemy's lies by abiding in God's Truth (the Word).

Finally, speaking and living a life of truthfulness is the belt of truth. Speaking and living a life of truthfulness does several things for the Christian soldier:

(1) it keeps us from flapping about from one thing to another, from being tossed to and fro by every attack of the enemy;

(2) it keeps us from becoming entangled with the affairs of this life; and

(3) it supports us in the battles and trials of life.

Often times, we as Christians can be deceived by the devil into believing he is telling us the truth. But we know that the devil is the father of lies and the truth is not in him (John 8:44). The enemy has a targeted attack for every individual Christian; he knows what thing causes each of us to stumble and fall short of God's Glory. The over-arching principle present in all of Satan's attacks toward us is DECEPTION. It is the enemy who causes us to question God's Word. The way of escape from the devil's snare is for truth to reveal itself and do its work. Therefore, daily bible reading is the best antidote to the lies of the enemy.

One of the enemy's common tactics in telling us lies is to put the lies in the first person. For example, the thought may come "My life isn't worth living" or "God doesn't care about me." The devil knows we are far more likely to believe his lies if we acknowledge the thoughts as our own and start speaking them out of our own mouths. DO NOT FALL FOR IT! Instead, speak the TRUTH! "God is faithful, who will not suffer you to be tempted above that ye are able; but will with the temptation also make a way to escape, that ye may be able to bear it."

We cannot trust what our eyes see; what our ears hear; what our fingers feel. We need a light so that we do not lean to our own understanding and acknowledge God in all of our ways. *Proverbs 3:5-6*. Our feelings do not have intellect. Our feelings can lead us down paths we should not take; paths that are not aligned with God's Promises for our lives. Trust God and His Word.

There are times when the Belt of Truth that you wear around your waist might crack. You might do something that you shouldn't have done. Do not attempt to patch up the belt on your own or try to hide the break from view and pretend that nothing untoward has happened. Though this might be the only mistake that you have made in ages it is enough to leave you open to the enemy's assaults and a quick fix could prove extremely dangerous. Simply acknowledge the belt is broken and ask God to fix it. This consists of admitting you made a mistake and seeking God's pardon. If you do this with no attempt at a cover up you take away all power the enemy has over you.

To know truth is good but we as Christians must embrace truth at all times and agree to continually grow in it. We can count on the Word of God as absolute truth and use the scriptures as a trusted moral compass. "For it is written, 'Man shall not live by bread alone, but by every word that proceeds from the Mouth of God.'" *Matthew 4:4*. The sign of the Christian soldier is the truth of God that holds everything together. Isn't that great to know today? Aren't you glad to know that God and God alone can possess and give enough pure truth to embrace all men?? I know I am glad to know that.

No matter what confronts us in our daily lives, we can rely on the Truth of God's Word to be rock solid for out Christian faith. The better we know the content of the Bible, the better equipped we will be to distinguish truth from untruth. Having a solid grasp of the Truth contained within the Bible enables us to confidently hang the other elements of our Christian faith on a solid foundation.

In conclusion, the opposite of truth is lies and error, which lead to bondage. Build your house on the solid rock of God's Truth.

Since truth is so important to our temporary physical lives, how much more important is it to our eternal souls?

_____

_____

_____

_____

_____

_____

_____

_____

BREASTPLATE OF RIGHTEOUSNESS – PURE HEART AND ALIVE SPIRIT

The breastplate was a central part of the Roman soldier's armor, providing protection to them for their torsos. In this area, vital organs exist, such as the heart and lungs. Without a breastplate, a soldier goes into battle asking for death because any attack can become fatal. Additionally, if the belt was loosened, the breastplate could slip right off. However, with a sturdy breastplate, those very same attacks become ineffective, useless, and certainly not fatal.

Without **righteousness**, we leave ourselves open to almost certain death. To be righteous is to do what is right in God's Eyes. God's Commandments are righteousness. Righteousness is upright living that aligns with the expectations of God.

To "put on" the breastplate of righteousness, we must first have our BELT OF TRUTH on firmly in place. Without truth, our righteousness will be based upon our own attempts to impress God. We "put it on" by seeking God and His Righteousness above everything else (*Matt. 6:33*). Putting on and wearing the breastplate of righteousness creates a lifestyle of putting into practice what we believe in our hearts. As our lives become conformed to the image of Christ, our choices become more righteous and these Godly choices also protect us from further temptation and deception.

Many times, the devil will try to bring up your past and make you feel like you are not good enough but your breastplate of righteousness is your trusty defense. Righteousness is God's double-sided protection for the Christian. It defends our conscience from all the wounds inflicted by past sin and failures and also keeps us from the constant array of temptations and lust that desire to inflict more harm on us.

Just as a Roman soldier's breastplate protected his organs such as his heart and lungs, our spiritual breastplate of righteousness also protects our heart. God wants our whole hearts and nothing less. *Proverbs 4:23* says "keep thy heart with all diligence; for out of it are the issues of life." The breastplate of righteousness is so critical that there approximately 900 Bible verses referring to the spiritual heart.

However, when our armor is abused or worn incorrectly, it can malfunction and be susceptible to the enemy's evil tactics. Likewise, there are several factors that can (and do) interfere with the effectiveness of our breastplate of righteousness. Carelessness, unbelief, abusing grace, and disobedience can hinder our ability to stand firm and defeat the enemy in our lives. When we live a lifestyle contrary to God's Word, we invite the enemy into our lives and give him free range. Unrighteousness is the enemy's invitation.

We can pray and ask God to help us live righteous lives, but we must also put into practice what we pray to God. If you are praying against the enemy and still living unrighteous, your prayers will not be effective. Align your life with God's Word. This is something every believer struggles with at some point in their walk with Christ – practicing what they "preach."

The Bible does not say that weapons will not form against us. However, the Bible (the TRUTH) does tell us that those weapons will not prosper (*Isaiah 54:17*) because we have "put on" our breastplate of righteousness to guard our vital spiritual organs.

One thing we must remember is that "we don't wrestle against flesh and blood, but against principalities, against powers, against the rulers of the darkness of this age, against spiritual hosts of wickedness in the heavenly places." *Ephesians 6:10-12*. With this in mind, it is futile to fight using human logic and human strength, and it is necessary to see the real enemy, not the person or people Satan has used to break hearts and wound or kill a human's spirit.

To "put on" the breastplate of righteousness, us Christians must learn to live without sin and to know who we are in Christ. We should be bold in asking God for help, protection and provision. We, as believers, should pray and intercede for ourselves and on behalf of others, and be willing to take off worldly layers and replace them with the good things of God. In doing so, the breastplate of righteousness will keep hearts pure and spirits alive.

How sturdy is your breastplate of righteousness? How easy can the devil influence your decisions? How can you tighten your breastplate of righteousness to adequately protect your vital spiritual organs?

_____

_____

_____

_____

_____

_____

_____

_____

Prayer: Lord, thank you for this week's lesson on the belt of truth and breastplate of righteousness.

I know that Your Word is the truth and light of the world, despite the lies Satan may tell me. I pray that my belt stays fastened so that I can stand against the evil one. Lord, when I do fall, help me to come to you and admit my faults and not try to patch up my sins, leaving me open and vulnerable to the attacks of the evil one. Lord, help me to study Your Word – the Truth – and stay in the Truth. I pray that you take away anything that is not like You, Lord and help me to be a model Christian for You and Your Glory.

And, Lord, I pray that my breastplate of righteousness is fastened tight to protect my vital spiritual organs so that the enemy's attacks against me will be futile. Lord, help me to remember that although weapons may form against me, they will not prosper! And also help me to remember that I do not wrestle against flesh and blood. The devil is the true enemy and when I am aware of that, I can adequately and accurately fight off the enemy, with the truth (Your Word).

And at the end of the day, I pray that I have the victory in Your Name. In Jesus name I pray. Amen.

Week 11: Shoes of Peace and Shield of Faith

<u>Days 71 – 77 -</u> _____
Songs: **"For Your Glory" by Tasha Cobbs**

"Victory" by Yolanda Adams

Ephesians 6:10-18
10 Finally, be strong in the Lord and in his mighty power. 11 Put on the full armor of God, so that you can take your stand against the devil's schemes. 12 For our struggle is not against flesh and blood, but against the rulers, against the authorities, against the powers of this dark world and against the spiritual forces of evil in the heavenly realms. 13 Therefore put on the full armor of God, so that when the day of evil comes, you may be able to stand your ground, and after you have done everything, to stand. 14 Stand firm then, with the belt of truth buckled around your waist, with the breastplate of righteousness in place, ***15 and with your feet fitted with the readiness that comes from the gospel of peace. 16 In addition to all this, take up the shield of faith, with which you can extinguish all the flaming arrows of the evil one.*** *17 Take the helmet of salvation and the sword of the Spirit, which is the word of God. 18 And pray in the Spirit on all occasions with all kinds of prayers and requests. With this in mind, be alert and always keep on praying for all the Lord's people.* **Ephesians 6:10-18.**

SHOES OF THE PREPARATION OF THE GOSPEL OF PEACE-GO OUT AND SPREAD THE GOOD NEWS

Can you imagine a fully-armed soldier without shoes on? What about yourself? Picture yourself completely dressed – shirt, pants, jacket, jewelry – but no shoes. How awkward is that picture? Just by the appearance, anyone can tell that something is missing.

However, this goes far beyond mere awkwardness – a shoeless soldier can run into real troubles in the heat of battle. Although it can be something so small as a stick or a rock, but to a bare foot, that can cause severe pain. Simply put, shoes allow us to step freely and without fear while we turn our full attention to the battle at hand.

Spiritually, the shoes of the preparation of the Gospel of Peace allow us to walk in Christ and announce the Good News. With our shoes on, we are ready to go out and spread the Good News to others. Not only that but we need to be at peace with God – the firm foundation beneath our feet. Have you ever heard the saying "No Jesus, No Peace; Know Jesus, Know Peace." Once we abide in Christ, then the peace of God will become a reality to us.

We must always be prepared for what may come our way to throw us off. In the army of God, there are times of rest and refreshment, but there is NEVER a time for complacency. We cannot allow our guards to be let down and get comfortable because it would be far too easy for the enemy to attack.

What we wear on our feet determines our stability and mobility. What shoes we wear affects how far we can walk or run comfortably. The wrong choice of footwear can cripple us, slow us down, and make us drop out of the line of march. Think about it. We can purchase an inexpensive pair of shoes but they will not last as long as a more expensive pair nor will they feel as comfortable.

When we get footsore, we slow down and limp. The word we use for this condition is – lame. We also use this word lame to describe a person who is weak, inarticulate, or whose power is diminished by his position, e.g. lame duck. An argument that is weak and has no merit is called lame.

The enemy harasses the lame, and takes advantage of their weakness. A lame Christian limps along in life, subject to attack, unstable and almost immobile, getting nowhere in his spiritual journey. Because he is lagging behind, and not keeping up with his commanding officer, he is vulnerable to attack. He suffers from neglecting to pay attention to his basic form of locomotion – what shoes he wears on his feet.

Lameness is the result of wearing shoes that are inappropriate for the journey. Sore feet occur when we choose our footwear for appearance and for fashion rather than for comfort and utility. Can you imagine a soldier going into battle wearing dress shoes, or high heels? Yet we can walk through the hours of each day being more concerned for appearance, what looks cool, what blends in, than with substance and integrity.

When we choose appearance and current fashion in order to meet our needs of acceptance and self esteem, we are vulnerable to spiritual attack and injury. We are relying on our being able to impress others for our peace of mind. This is why clothes and footwear are so important to us from childhood on. They help demonstrate what identity we want to project to others.

A strong motivation in our lives is the desire to want to look good in the eyes of others. We want to impress our peers. Our peace is often dependent on that acceptance. Some people want to stand out and be different. Others want to blend in. Either way we are tempted to opt for inappropriate footwear – footwear that causes us to be unstable and immobile, sitting ducks for the enemy of our souls.

What is the appropriate footwear for the battle of life – for the time of testing that we experience in this life? It is the readiness that comes from the gospel of peace. The gospel of peace prepares us to be ready to deal with what life throws at us. If we are clothed with the gospel of peace, we are ready for what life may bring. What is this gospel of peace?

First, it is the good news of peace with God. St. Paul argues that, as a result of being "justified by faith [i.e. having put on the breastplate of the righteousness of Christ], we have peace with God through our Lord Jesus Christ, through whom we have gained access by faith into this grace in which we now stand." *Romans 5:1-2*.

If we are to fight the enemy of our souls, and win the victory, we have to be clear about our relationship with God. We need to be clear about our sinfulness, our need for salvation, for forgiveness, for acceptance before God. We need the stability of a harmonious relationship with God if we are to stand firm. There should be nothing that comes between God and us. We are to keep short accounts with God –

confessing our sins and accepting his cleansing each day. It is what Jesus did for us on the Cross that purchased our peace with God. As we appropriate that peace by faith in Christ, we gain access into a relationship that ends our alienation from God.

The gospel of peace is also peace within. We need peace within ourselves if we are to win the victory. Our stability comes from confidence about God being able to take care of us in daily life. If we are guilty, anxious, and worried about the issues that can distress us, we cannot defeat fear and despair. God's Peace is an inner tranquility and calmness of the soul.

A person who is shod with the gospel of peace will not be worried, anxious, troubled or frantic. Fear defeats us even before we start to run the race. God's Peace (1) gives us a firm grip which we need in a world that is not firm; (2) gives us stability; (3) allows us to keep our footing when everything around us is swirling; and (4) keeps us sane. I went through a very rough patch (after asking God for patience) whereby I was frustrated – mentally, emotionally, and even spiritually. However, I remembered to "put on" the WHOLE Armor of God and I recalled God's Peace. People around me who knew what was going on in my life made statements like "I don't know how you are so calm about your situation. If it were me, I would have gone crazy by now." And I ministered to them by saying "When you know that God's got you, then you don't worry about it; you let God fight your battles." That is how I know I have God's Peace – I don't allow my circumstances predict my actions/reactions.

The gospel of peace has to be put on, just as shoes need to be put on and laced up. It requires us being willing to wear it every day. We put on these shoes of the gospel of peace through prayer.

Are your shoes raggedy and worn or are they still in perfect condition? What does the wear and tear on your shoes indicate about your position in the Army of God?

_____

_____

_____

_____

_____

_____

_____

_____

SHIELD OF FAITH- FAITH OVER FEAR

The Roman shield, the *scutum*, was made from bonded wood strips and covered with leather. The shield was semicircular so that any missiles thrown at the soldier would be deflected to one side. Iron or brass rims fitted along the edges of the shield, and a leather strap fastened to the back. The shield has a metal projection in the center, which was used to stun or wind an opponent, easing the soldier's subsequent strike with his sword.

The Romans were feared for their effective military tactics and battle formations. One formation in particular was known as the "tortoise," so named because the soldiers' shields would protect the men like a shell protects a tortoise. The front row of soldiers held their shields in front of them, edge to edge; soldiers on the flanks held their shields to the side. Lastly, troops in the middle balanced their shields on their helmets. As long as the soldiers held together this way, the enemy would have trouble defeating them. Even the enemy's fiery darts (arrows tipped with a flammable liquid then set on fire) were ineffective against the Roman shields because the Romans drenched their leather-covered shields with water before going to battle.

When you "put on" the shield, you essentially are saying that you have faith in God. Faith is taking God at His Word without ever having to visibly see any evidence. You believe and trust God – both must be present to make faith.

At some point in our lives, we will face difficult situations and temptations of the enemy. The good thing about this is that the shield of faith is the protection God has provided to get us through those tests. In temptation, the enemy will try to make us believe that sin can provide a better life than God can. In reality, however, there is no better life than one with God. "Putting on" our shield of faith will allow us to deflect that attack. In a difficult situation, the enemy will use fear to try and get our eyes off of Jesus Christ. However, "putting on" our shield of faith will deflect that attack as well. Fear is the complete opposite of faith. When we have faith, we know that nothing is too hard for God (*Jeremiah 32:27*). Without faith, it is impossible to please God (*Hebrews 11:6*).

It is so important to have faith in God. Instead of allowing life's circumstances to dictate your perception of God, allow God's Word to tell you the truth about Him. As you read and hear truth about God from His Word, your faith will increase, for faith comes by hearing, and hearing by the Word of God (Romans 10:17).

What does faith do? Faith (1) saves, (2) justifies, (3) stabilizes, (4) strengthens, (5) sings, and (6) sends us out.

First, salvation is not by works or deeds. It is by believing. Second, when we are justified, we are made right in the sight of God. Third, faith makes us steadfast when the battle is raging hot and gives us courage to stand when the flesh desires to run.

Fourth, faith strengthens us. God has the power for our lives, IF we connect to Him. It is only through God we can do all things, for, we can do nothing in ourselves. This is very important to remember, especially when God has performed miracles in our lives. We must remember that it was not our own doing but God's Power that performed those good works in our lives.

Fifth, we have a song in our hearts in the midst of darkness – physical sufferings, loss of possession, hardships, and grief. It was faith that made Paul sing at the midnight hour. They were not singing because they feared the darkness or the hand of the Roman government. They sang because their hearts were full of faith and they knew that God was with them. Take this motto for your life: "Rejoice evermore." Rest on the promises. Rejoice in the Lord. Again, I say, Rejoice! *Philippians 4:4.*

Finally, it is faith that makes us messengers and witnesses for Christ. What God has done for us, He can (and will) do for others. We can (and should) have faith in the power of Christ to save to the utter-most. He will save if you only believe and trust in Him.

By wielding the shield of faith in knowing who our God is and what His Word says, we can overcome all the fiery darts of the wicked.

We must also remember that faith without works is useless. *James 2:17.* We may have faith in God but God also requires us to work our faith and not just speak our faith in Him. Faith relates to the activity of the believer – give your faith a job! Active faith is a shield! Faith is not what you say you believe. Rather, it is what you say you believe in action. Faith is when you act like God is telling the truth.

Let us give our faith a job – have active faith. It is then, and only then, we have actually "put on" the SHIELD OF FAITH.

What is your concept of God? Do you perceive God as far and distant? Or do you perceive Him to be big, powerful, and directly involved in your life? Will your faith in God and His Word stand the test?

_____

_____

_____

_____

_____

_____

_____

Prayer: Lord, thank you for this week's lesson on Shoes of Peace and Shield of Faith. Help us to "put on" the shoes of peace and the shield of faith so that no matter what the enemy throws at us we will be able to withstand the evil tactics and have faith that God will bring us through and out of it. Lord, please don't allow my shoes to become so worn that I get foot sores and limp through battle. Help me to remain strong in You. And when I don't feel like I can go on, give me faith in You that I can. Your Word says all I need is faith the size of a mustard seed and I would be able to move mountains and I believe and trust in Your Word. I pray that I remain faithful to You and continue to have that type of faith. Help me to activate my faith and not just speak about my faith. It is in Jesus name I do pray. Amen.

Week 12: Helmet of Salvation and Sword of the Spirit

<u>Days 78 – 84 -</u>_____
Songs: **"Pressure" by Jonathan McReynolds**

"Victory" by Yolanda Adams

Ephesians 6:10-18
10 Finally, be strong in the Lord and in his mighty power. 11 Put on the full armor of God, so that you can take your stand against the devil's schemes. 12 For our struggle is not against flesh and blood, but against the rulers, against the authorities, against the powers of this dark world and against the spiritual forces of evil in the heavenly realms. 13 Therefore put on the full armor of God, so that when the day of evil comes, you may be able to stand your ground, and after you have done everything, to stand. 14 Stand firm then, with the belt of truth buckled around your waist, with the breastplate of righteousness in place, 15 and with your feet fitted with the readiness that comes from the gospel of peace. 16 In addition to all this, take up the shield of faith, with which you can extinguish all the flaming arrows of the evil one. 17 Take the helmet of salvation and the sword of the Spirit, which is the word of God. 18 And pray in the Spirit on all occasions with all kinds of prayers and requests. With this in mind, be alert and always keep on praying for all the Lord's people. **Ephesians 6:10-18.**

HELMET OF SALVATION – GET YOUR MIND RIGHT

A Roman soldier's helmet protected a soldier's skull and neck from enemy blows and falling debris. The helmet included two hinged sidepieces to protect the cheekbones and jaw. Helmets were often lined inside with sponge or felt for the sake of comfort.

The helmet of salvation guards our minds. When we do not guard our minds, we are vulnerable to the enemy's lie that life is not worth living, and all other lies the enemy can fill our minds with. The enemy will fill our minds with discouragement, doubt and defeat; pointing out our failures and try to get us to focus on the negative, and attack our hope in

God. Do not allow the enemy to do that. This is why we must get our minds right!

Many of Satan's attacks happen in the mind. The devil can flash evil and lewd thoughts in our minds, hoping that we will entertain his thoughts and commit sin. Let us not be ignorant of the enemy's attempts to get our thoughts preoccupied with the lusts and cares of this world.

There are strongholds raised in our minds that stand against the Word of God. *2 Cor. 10:4*. The enemy wants to erect a partition in our minds to section off what God would have us to do. We MUST have a strong mind to work against the enemy's tactics against our minds.

Because of the power of the cross, our enemy no longer has any hold on us. He knows that, but he also knows that most of God's children do not know that – or, at least they do not live as if they know. We must learn to keep our helmets buckled so that his fiery missiles do not lodge in our thoughts and set us on fire. Through this helmet of salvation, we can "destroy arguments and every lofty opinion raised against the knowledge of God, and take every thought captive to obey Christ." (2 Cor. 10:5). There are several actions us believers can take to keep our helmets fastened and functioning:

First, we can renew our minds. We can do this by allowing the truth of God's Word to wipe out anything contrary to it – wash away the world's filth, lies and confusion from our minds and adopt God's perspective.

Second, we can reject doubts that arise from circumstances. We are sensory creatures and what we cannot fathom with our five senses, we tend to disregard. It is impossible to have faith and doubt simultaneously. With the helmet of salvation firmly in place, we can choose to believe what appears impossible through our faith in God.

Third, we can keep an eternal perspective. When life crashes in around us, we must remember to look to the hill from which our help comes from (Ps. 121:1).

Fourth, we can remember that victory is already accomplished. When choosing sin is no longer an option for us because we recognize ourselves to be "new creatures" then we effectively cut off many avenues of failure.

Finally, we can find all of our hope in Him. Our helmet is most effective when we treasure what it represents. The salvation Jesus purchased for us cannot share the place of important in our hearts with earthly things. When pleasing the Lord is our supreme delight, we eliminate many of Satan's lures and render his evil suggestions powerless.

As we wear the helmet of salvation every day, our minds become more insulated against the suggestions, desires, and traps the enemy lays for us. We choose to guard our minds from excessive worldly influence and instead think on things that honor Christ. In doing so, we wear our salvation as a protective helmet that will "guard our hearts and minds in Christ Jesus."

Salvation is not just about redemption; it is also a defensive, protective device. Our salvation is our liberation. We are supposed to walk in the liberation from God. Doesn't it feel great to be liberated by God through salvation?! We have salvation that frees us and keeps us free!

How does the helmet of salvation guard a Christian's mind? Is your mind guarded?

_____

_____

_____

_____

_____

_____

SWORD OF THE SPIRIT – THE LIVING WORD OF GOD

The Roman sword was crafted of iron. Blacksmiths hardened the iron by coating the red-hot sword blade with coal dust, thus forming a hard carbon coating on the blade. Sword handles were made of iron, ivory, bone, or wood. The Romans used their swords both offensively and defensively.

Offensively, the sword was used to attack and counter-attack an enemy until the weapon seriously wounded or killed the assailant. Defensively, the sword, along with other pieces of the armor, enabled the soldier to deflect the enemy's blows.

Our sword, is the Word of God – the Bible. The Word is made alive by the Holy Spirit, causing it to be filled with divine energy and ability. With this power, the Word is able to cut down the strongholds of Satan. By actively using the Word, we have huge advantage over our enemies. Unfortunately, though, most of us fail to wield our swords. Instead, we display it as a decorative shelf piece, giving the enemy a greater advantage.

Learning to use our sword requires many hours of practice (study). We shouldn't wait until the heat of battle to learn to use our sword. Just as the Roman sword was used offensively and defensively, so should our sword (the Word) be used. Offensively, we should hide God's Word in our heart, rooting out sin, and strengthen our inner man with God's Promises before the enemy attacks. Used defensively, we deflect the devil's lies, doubts, and temptations with the truth of the Word.

Why is the SWORD OF THE SPIRIT so critical? It is unique because (1) it is the only piece of armor that Paul actually describes; and (2) it is the only offensive weapon. The other pieces of the armor were all defensive weapons. Understanding this is to know that withstanding the attacks of the enemy, is not just defensive; but offensive also – being proactive to the attacks of the enemy.

Sometimes, it will feel like the enemy is right in our face. When we feel like this, this is when we need the SWORD OF THE SPIRIT.

How much practice do you have using your sword? Do you wait until you are in a heated battle to learn to use your sword?

_____

_____

_____

_____

_____

_____

_____

_____

Prayer: Lord, thank you for this week's lesson on the Helmet of Salvation and the Sword of the Spirit. Help me to "put on" and KEEP ON the Armor of God so that I can withstand the attacks from the enemy. Help me to keep my mind on You. Help me to fight against the enemy's fiery darts and keep my mind stayed on You. Lord, help me to use both my defensive and offensive weapons against the enemy when he attacks. Help me to remember that the SWORD OF THE SPIRIT is YOUR WORD. I pray that I "put on" the WHOLE armor every single day of my life, and not just when it is convenient for me. In Jesus name. Amen.

Week 13: PRAYER

Days 85 – 91 - _____
Songs: **"Rejoice" by B. Simmons feat. Victoria C. Duhon and Darnisha Edwards**

"Victory" by Yolanda Adams

This week, we will pray specifically. It is known that prayers of the righteous availeth much and there is nothing too hard for God. *James 5:16* and *Jeremiah 32:27*. Each day, we will pray for something different and, in your own time, pray for those specific prayer requests you may have.

Ephesians 6:10-18
10 Finally, be strong in the Lord and in his mighty power. 11 Put on the full armor of God, so that you can take your stand against the devil's schemes. 12 For our struggle is not against flesh and blood, but against the rulers, against the authorities, against the powers of this dark world and against the spiritual forces of evil in the heavenly realms. 13 Therefore put on the full armor of God, so that when the day of evil comes, you may be able to stand your ground, and after you have done everything, to stand. 14 Stand firm then, with the belt of truth buckled around your waist, with the breastplate of righteousness in place, 15 and with your feet fitted with the readiness that comes from the gospel of peace. 16 In addition to all this, take up the shield of faith, with which you can extinguish all the flaming arrows of the evil one. 17 Take the helmet of salvation and the sword of the Spirit, which is the word of God. 18 ***And pray in the Spirit on all occasions with all kinds of prayers and requests. With this in mind, be alert and always keep on praying for all the Lord's people****.* **Ephesians 6:10-18.**

The Bible gives us a guide on how to pray:
In this manner, therefore, pray: Our Father in heaven, Hallowed by Your name. Your kingdom come. Your will be done on earth as it is in heaven. Give us this day our daily bread. And forgive us our debts, as we forgive our debts, as we forgive our debtors. And do not lead us into temptation, but deliver us from the evil one. For Yours in the kingdom

and the power and the glory forever. Amen. Matthew 6:9-13.

Date:_____

Pray for FRANs – Friends, Relatives, Associates and Neighbors.

Lord, today I say a special prayer for a special group of people – my FRANs. I pray for them individually and collectively, that You bless them and keep them.

I pray for my FRIENDS – that You will make them friendly, not only to me, but to all they come in contact with.

I pray for my RELATIVES that they do not allow the ways of this wicked world to come between and mess up what You have ordained. Remind us that blood is thicker than water and we are connected by blood. Help us to always look past each other's faults and forgive one another.

I pray for my ASSOCIATES that they do not take advantage of me because I am a Christian. Lord, lead them to do right in Your Eyes.

Lord, I pray for my NEIGHBORS. I pray that they remember the importance of sticking together with the neighborhood. Allow us to work together to keep our neighborhood safe and free from hurt, harm and danger.

Finally, I pray for this group collectively. I pray for their relationship with You – that they grow in their walk with You. I pray for their hearts and minds that they are aligned with You and Your Word. I pray they do not allow the enemy to attack their mind by putting on and keeping on the helmet of salvation and trusting in You. I pray that they practice the Fruit of the Holy Spirit - . *(1) **charity/love**; (2) joy; (3) peace; (4) patience; (5) kindness; (6) goodness; (7) faithfulness; (8) gentleness; and (9) self-control.*

All of these things I ask in Jesus name. Amen.

Write your own prayer here:

_____

_____

_____

_____

Date:_____

Pray for the universe – world/nation/local leaders, world/nation/local peace, world/nation/local issues, etc.

Lord, thank you for this day. A day I have never seen and a day I will never see again. Thank you for Your Grace and Your Mercy. Lord, you said that when two or three would gather together in Your Name, then You would be present with them. So, right now, I come, uniting myself with many Christians throughout the world, who, though separate, are gathered together in another sense to pray to You. I trust that you are with me now as I pray for this universe You created – praying for world peace, world leaders, and issues that plague this world. Praying for healing and belief and trust in You, Lord. I know all things are possible if I believe in You so that is what I am going to do.

Lord, thank you for Your Goodness and Mercy to this nation. Thank you for giving us blessings far beyond what we deserve and protecting us from disasters we so deserve. We know that all is not right with America but we pray that You continue to watch over and protect. America needs moral and spiritual renewal to help us meet the many problems we face. Convict us of all sin. Help us to turn to You in repentance and in faith. Set our feet on the path of Your Righteousness and Peace.

We pray for our nation's leaders. Give them the wisdom to know what is right, and the courage to do it, even when their colleagues expect them to do wrong. Remind them that things cannot be both politically and biblically correct. Remind them that You are the way, the truth, and the life. Psalm 33:12 says "blessed is the nation whose God is The Lord." Lord, bless this nation because You are Lord of lords!

May this be a new era for America, as we humble ourselves and acknowledge You alone as our Savior and Lord.

And, Lord, bless my city – its leaders and citizens. Help the leaders to make the right decision and not be afraid to worry about what their colleagues may think. Let them use their active faith in You and not be encouraged by the enemy to do wrong.

In Jesus name. Amen.

Write your own prayer here:

_____

_____

_____

_____

Date:_____
Pray for the less fortunate.

Lord, I come to you only as I know how – humbly. I thank you for those things You have given me and those things You have shielded me from. Thank you for Your Grace and Mercy. I pray for those who are less fortunate – physically and spiritually.

I pray that those who are physically less fortunate that you bless them with Your Promises. And then those who are spiritually less fortunate that you fill them with your presence. They shall not have peace until they have Your Peace within them. They shall run to You just as they are and make a commitment to You and Your Word. I pray they repent their sins ad ask for Your Forgiveness and remain faithful to You. It is then that they shall be blessed by you. It is in Jesus name I pray. Amen.

Write your own prayer here:

_____

_____

_____

_____

Date:_____

Pray for sick and shut-in. Pray for those persons (co-workers, neighbors, family members) you know who are suffering from sickness and diseases. Pray for total healing in their bodies.

Lord, we pray that You lay Your Healing Hands on all who are sick. We beg You to have compassion on those who are suffering so that they may be delivered from their sickness and disease.

We know that You are the Doctor of all doctors and You know all about us. Not only heal their physical bodies, but heir their spiritual and emotional bodies. Let them know that You wont put more on them than they can bear. I pray they find comfort in knowing that You love them no matter what condition they may be in. Let Your Will be done. In Jesus name. Amen.

Write your own prayer here:

_____

_____

_____

_____

Date: _____
Pray for peace in your life.

Lord, give me Your Peace. Give me confidence in the depths of danger. Give me hope when I am surrounded by fear. Still my worries, calm the anxieties pressing in on me from the world we live in.

Lord, reassure me that You are with me when I feel alone. Ease my doubting. Guide my search for peace so that I may not seek it where it is not to be found. For we know that You will keep us in perfect peace if our mind is stayed on You and when we trust You. In Jesus name. Amen.

Write your own prayer here:

_____

_____

_____

_____

Date: _____
Pray for discernment and wisdom for your life.

Almighty God, the fountain of all wisdom, You know our necessities before we ask and our ignorance in asking. Lord, have compassion on our weakness, and mercifully give us those things which for our unworthiness we dare not, and for our blindness we cannot ask. Lord, direct our minds and bodies throughout this day and make us holy.

Guide us in your gentle mercy, for we cannot do Your Will by ourselves. Bring us back to You and fill our minds with Your Wisdom. Guide us with kindness and govern us with love. Give the spirit of wisdom to those You have called to lead Your Church. May the growth of Your people in holiness be the eternal joy of our shepherds. In Jesus name. Amen.

Write your own prayer here:

_____

_____

_____

_____

Date:_____

Pray for your career and "social" life.

Lord, lead me to make choices that bring You glory and allow me to experience the life You intended for me to live. By Your Spirit, help us to know what is right and to be eager in doing Your Will.

Lord, bless my career. Allow me to be a light to my co-workers so they may come to know You and acknowledge You as their Savior and Lord. Let those who do not know You to turn his/her ears to You. Do not withhold Your Mercy from them. Promote me in my career, Lord. And I pray that when I am promoted, I remember to give You all the glory and honor because it is because of You I received that promotion/increase.

And, Lord, bless my social life in that it is pleasing to You. Do not allow me to go places You do not want me to go. Convict me when I go places, say things, do things that are not according to Your Will and do not bring You glory. In Jesus name. Amen.

Write your own prayer here:

_____

_____

Date: _____

Pray for yourself and your household. Whatever you may be needing today, ask God for it. *I found this prayer online and thought it was all-inclusive.*

Lord, let me be just what they need. If they need someone to trust, let me be trustworthy. If they need sympathy, let me sympathize. If they need love, let me love in full measure. Let me not anger easily. Permit my justice to be tempted in Your mercy. When I stand before them, Lord, let me look strong and good and honest and loving. Let me be as strong and good and honest and loving as I look to them. Permit me to teach only the truth and help me to inspire so that learning does not cease at the classroom door. Let the lessons they learn make their lives fruitful and happy, and, Lord, let me bring them to You. Teach them, through me, to love You. Finally, permit me to learn the lessons they teach. In Jesus name. Amen.

Write your own prayer here:

_____

_____

_____

_____

Final Prayer:
Lord, thank you for this week on PRAYER, the most important piece of the Armor of God. Help us to remember that prayer is communication between us and You. Lord, mercifully receive the prayers of Your people who call upon You, an grant that they may know and understand what things they ought to do. Lord, please have grace and power faithfully to accomplish them; through Jesus Christ our Lord, who lives

and reigns with You and the Holy Spirit. And remind us to REJOICE and have a "YET PRAISE!"

Also, thank you Lord for this 13-week bible study. It required me to search every part of my soul and to dig deep within and I thank you for that. In this, I was able to remove those things that are not like You. I was reminded that You are always with me, no matter what condition I may be in. I was reminded of many other things – too many to name. I pray that You continue to work in and through me and that You will get all of the glory.

In Jesus name. Amen.

Final Writing:
What step(s) will you take to maintain what you have learned from this bible study?

_____

_____

_____

_____

_____

_____

_____

_____

_____

_____

_____

_____

Below you will find a list of scriptures to memorize each week beginning January 1. I pray that the 13-week bible study has blessed you and has drawn each of you closer to God and has given you the desire to be even closer to Him. If it helps, write the verses down daily to memorize these Bible scriptures.

Remember, you get out what you put in. Don't forget the Fruit of the Holy Spirit and don't forget to "PUT ON" the WHOLE Armor of God so that you can withstand the enemy's attacks against you and your life. What God has for you, it is for you but you have to trust and believe that He will do just what He said He would do!

Week 1 (1/1): Psalm 119:105 "Your word is a lamp to my feet and a light for my path."

Week 2 (1/8): Proverbs 3:5 "Trust in the LORD with all your heart and lean not on your own understanding."

Week 3 (1/15): 1 Thesalonians 5:17 "Pray without ceasing."

Week 4 (1/22): 2 Corinthians 5:17 "Therefore, if anyone is in Christ, he is a new creation; the old has gone, the new has come!"

Week 5 (1/29): 1 Corinthians 16:13 "Be on your guard; stand firm in the faith; be courageous; be strong."

Week 6 (2/5): Colossians 3:23 "And whatever you do, do it heartily, as to the Lord and not to men."

Week 7 (2/12): Luke 12:34 "For where your treasure is, there will your heart be also."

Week 8 (2/19): Philippians 4:13 "I can do all things through Christ who strengthens me."

Week 9 (2/26): Philippians 4:19 "My God shall supply all your need according to his riches in glory by Christ Jesus."

Week 10 (3/4): Jeremiah 29:11 "'For I know the plans I have for you,' declares the Lord, 'plans to prosper you and not to harm you, plans to give you hope and a future.'"

Week 11 (3/11): Isaiah 26:3 "You keep him in perfect peace whose mind is stayed on you, because he trusts in you."

Week 12 (3/18): James 1:5 "If any of you lacks wisdom, let him ask God who gives generously to all without reproach, and it will be given him."

Week 13 (3/25): Psalm 107:8 "Oh that men would praise the LORD for his goodness, and for his wonderful works to the children of men!"

Week 14 (4/1): Psalm 107:9 "For he satisfies the thirsty and fills the hungry with good things."

Week 15 (4/8): Galatians 6:7 "Do not be deceived: God cannot be mocked. A man reaps what he sows."

Week 16 (4/15): Psalm 23:1 "The LORD is my shepherd; I shall not want."

Week 17 (4/22): Psalm 23:6 "Surely goodness and mercy shall follow me all the days of my life, and I shall dwell in the house of the LORD forever."

Week 18 (4/29): Romans 8:28 "And we know that all things work together for good to them that love God, to them who are called according to his purpose."

Week 19 (5/6): Romans 8:31 "What shall we then say to these things? If God be for us, who can be against us?"

Week 20 (5/13): 1 Thessalonians 5:18 "In every thing give thanks for this is the will of God in Christ Jesus concerning you."

Week 21 (5/20): 2 Timothy 1:7 " For God hath not given us the spirit of fear; but of power, and of love, and of a sound mind."

Week 22 (5/27): John 14:6 "Jesus answered, 'I am the way and the truth and the life. No one comes to the Father except through me.'"

Week 23 (6/3): Romans 3:23 "For all have sinned and fall short of the glory of God."

Week 24 (6/10): Ephesians 2:8 "For by grace you have been saved through faith. And this is not your own doing; it is the gift of God."

Week 25 (6/17): Psalm 119:13 "I praise you because I am fearfully and wonderfully made; your works are wonderful, I know that full well."

Week 26 (6/24): Deuteronomy 6:5 "Love the LORD your God with all your heart and with all your soul and with all your strength."

Week 27 (7/1): Matthew 22:39 "Love your neighbor as yourself."

Week 28 (7/8): Philippians 4:6 "Do not be anxious about anything, but in every situation, by prayer and petition, with thanksgiving, present your requests to God."

Week 29 (7/15): Philippians 4:7 "And the peace of God, which transcends all understanding, will guard your hearts and your minds in Christ Jesus."

Week 30 (7/22): Proverbs 30:5 "Every word of God proves true; he is a shield to those who take refuge in him."

Week 31 (7/29): 1 Corinthians 10:31 "So whether you eat or drink or whatever you do, do it all for the glory of God."

Week 32 (8/5): Genesis 1:1 "In the beginning, God created the heavens and the earth."

Week 33 (8/12): Psalm 19:1 "The heavens declare the glory of God; the skies proclaim the work of his hands."

Week 34 (8/19): Psalm 1:6 "The LORD knows the way of the righteous, but the way of the wicked will perish."

Week 35 (8/26): Isaiah 43:1 "…Thus says the LORD…. 'Fear not, for I have redeemed you: I have called you by name, you are mine'….."

Week 36 (9/2): Isaiah 43:11 "I, I am the LORD, and besides me there is no savior."

Week 37 (9/9): Matthew 5:14 "You are the light of the world. A city set on a hill cannot be hidden."

Week 38 (9/16): Matthew 5:16 "Let your light shine before men, that they may see your good deeds and praise your Father in heaven."

Week 39 (9/23): Matthew 6:33 "Seek ye first the kingdom of God, and his righteousness; and all these things shall be added unto you."

Week 40 (9/30): Colossians 3:16 "Let the word of Christ dwell in you richly in all wisdom…"

Week 41 (10/7): Hebrews 13:8 "Jesus Christ is the same yesterday and today and forever."

Week 42 (10/14): Isaiah 40:31 "They that wait upon the LORD shall renew their strength; they shall mount up with wings as eagles; they shall run, and not be weary; and they shall walk, and not faint."

Week 43 (10/21): John 14:27 "Peace I leave with you; my peace I give you. I do not give to you as the world gives. Do not let your hearts be troubled and do not be afraid."

Week 44 (10/28): Psalm 37:4 "Commit your way to the LORD;trust in him and he will do this: He will make your righteous reward shine like the dawn."

Week 45 (11/4): John 16:24 "Ask, and you will receive, that your joy may be full."

Week 46 (11/11): John 3:16 "For God so loved the world that he gave his one and only Son, that whoever believes in him shall not perish but have eternal life."

Week 47 (11/18): 1 John 4:7 "Beloved, let us love one another, for love is of God; and everyone who loves is born of God and knows God."

Week 48 (11/25): Hebrews 10:24 "Let us think of ways to motivate one another to acts of love and good works."

Week 49 (12/2): Philippians 4:8 "Finally, brothers and sisters, whatever is true, whatever is noble, whatever is right, whatever is pure, whatever is lovely, whatever is admirable – if anything is excellent or praiseworthy – think about such things."

Week 50 (12/9): Job 36:11 "If they obey and serve him, They will spend the rest of their days in prosperity, and their years in contentment."

Week 51 (12/16): Isaiah 43:18 "Forget the former things; do not dwell on the past. See, I am doing a new thing!

Week 52 (12/23): Psalm 150:6 "Let everything that has breath praise the LORD. Praise the LORD."

73760725R00052

Made in the USA
Columbia, SC
21 July 2017